The **entrepreneur's** guide to launching a **fast, lean** and **profitable** online venture

ONLINE BUSINESS STARTUP

ROBIN WAITE

RƎTHINK PRESS

First published in Great Britain 2015
by Rethink Press (www.rethinkpress.com)

PRAISE

"Rob's book *Online Business Startup* is a refreshing read for any serious business owner. Rather than jumping right into tactics, he takes you by the hand and helps you explore what would actually benefit your business in a positive sense. Rob offers a great wealth of details so that business owners and entrepreneurs are empowered to make the right choices to gain visibility online. Highly recommended!"

Alex Rodríguez, author of Digital BACON:
Make Your Online Presence Irresistibly Attractive

"Rob in this book demystifies starting an online business and his approach is simple yet detailed and effective. An easy read that will help you to grow your online business."

Darshana Ubl – Businesswoman, Investor and
Spokesperson for Small Business

"Many new business owners get excited about starting their business, but fall into the trap of running before they can walk and set up a website without really understanding what their business is about. This book clearly explains the start up considerations all new businesses need to look into for setting up their online business, from thinking about their structure, name, logo, branding, finances through to eventually getting themselves online. It includes lots of useful tips and advice and is a fantastic guide for any entrepreneur."

Monica Or, Founder of Star Quality Hospitality Consultancy.

"I wish I had met Robin before I started my business as he would have minimised my stress and hard work significantly. This guy knows business strategy and the fine detail of getting set up in business. This book is a bible for the modern day business owner and covers absolutely everything that you need to know. I would certainly encourage anyone thinking of starting a business to read this book first. It is laid out in a simple format and very easy to understand. To make what seems to be a complicated process actually very simple, I have found that Robin's experience and guidance makes business life a whole lot easier. Thank you for this great book.

Paul Miller, Founder, Move Play Explore

"What a great book! Perfect for someone like me who's looking to start or grow an online business. All too often you find books on this subject are full of the 'what', but give very little of the 'how'. Not this one! Robin has been generous with his knowledge and expertise, offering great reminders of business basics, in addition to his step by step process for online success. If your dream is to have a 'fast, lean & profitable online business' and you're looking for easy to read, practical guidance, buy this book."

Marianne Page, Author of *Process to Profit*

"If you can't launch a successful online business after reading this book, then perhaps you should stick to your day job. The author doesn't beat around the bush and goes straight to the point; the book is concise and refreshingly easy to read."

Michael Serwa, Author of *From Good To Amazing:*
No Bullshit Tips for The Life You Always Wanted

CONTENTS

To my wife for her unending support, love and understanding. To my brother Matt, for his inspiration and energy. To Mum for her faith and encouragement. To my daughter Poppy for her smiles and happiness. And finally to Dad: you are remembered every day and always.

FOREWORD

As you are reading this, you may be wondering why you should read this book. I wish I had read this book seven years ago. I am going to tell you exactly how this book would have saved me thousands of pounds and sleepless nights if only I had read it when I was setting up my business.

To start with, I made a massive mistake when naming my company and I am still paying the price for this. *Online Business Startup* shows you what you must and mustn't do.

Secondly, I didn't have a capable web designer who cared what my business was about, he just wanted to build a website. I paid the price and found it hard to get clients to start with. This book explains clearly what you need to do, and will help you not make the mistakes I made.

Now let's talk about plans: have you got one? I had no plan when I started my business as I had no idea how to put one together. This book shows you how.

I then went on to spend many years learning how to market my business, and so much of what I searched for is included in this book, and it is clear and easy to understand.

And now the most difficult part of being online – your website. Who knew there was so much to know about who to choose to get to design and build your website, and what to pay, what to have on each page, etc. This book is the most comprehensive guide I have ever read about websites. This book answers every question you have when you are trying to get online, even the simple and scary one of 'what happens if my website designer gets run over by a bus?' If you want to know the answer to that, then pick up this book and read it!

And the cherry on the cake: it has a clear breakdown and simple explanation of how to market your business and website once you have launched it.

I will be recommending this book to every one of my clients, and I highly recommend it to you. It's an easy read for the online novice, and will stop you from wasting thousands of pounds and having sleepless nights like I used to.

Thank you to Robin for bringing this information together in an easy to read and succinct format.

Amanda C. Watts, Founder CEO, Clients in Abundance

INTRODUCTION

I hope he doesn't mind me recalling this story, but he's my brother and it's a fitting anecdote with which to kick things off. This book is dedicated to my brother Matt.

I am known amongst my family and circle of friends as the web geek who runs his own successful business. Therefore this makes me the one who knows everything about technology, IT, Emails, creating online businesses, you name it, I know it. This is a huge compliment because in reality I only specialise in online strategy. I have, however, managed to set up and run a successful web design and development agency for over a decade and for the most part have succeeded through an adventure of trial and error.

So, to my brother!

My wife and I had our family around for Sunday lunch, and during our coffee, post-roast, we got into a familiar topic of conversation about this great idea my brother had come up with for a 'website'. I understood the concept; he has asked me not to divulge his idea but it was a great concept that had led me to take pictures of random gloves abandoned in the pavement as I walked past them. They looked lonely on that rainy day; all they needed was to find their partner again and Matt had this great idea about how to reunite them, but, knowing what I do about websites, I started to drill down a bit.

'So, what's the revenue model for your business?'

'Well if you build me the website I'm sure we can make money out of it!'

I quizzed home further: 'Ok, well I would recommend maybe taking donations or perhaps an advertising revenue model, or merchandising, but you need visitors to your website first. How will you get lots of visitors?'

His short answer reflected that of many potential customers with great ideas, 'It's a great idea; if you build it surely we'll get thousands of hits.'

I have discussed all of the ins and outs of this idea with Matt; before embarking on any project with a new customer I always invite them in for a lengthy Strategy Session to get a better understanding of their business. I wanted to challenge him a little; after all, I wasn't going to do all of the donkey work!

'Ok, could you create a business plan for me? How are you going to market the website once I've built it?'

'I've got the idea – you build the website. It's what you do. I'll give you 50%.'

My final reply was something you might often hear on *Dragon's Den*.

'At the moment that's 50% of nothing. What if it never makes a penny? Perhaps you could write the business plan and we can go from there? Maybe come up with some projections for turnover and profit?'

Somewhere during this conversation the penny dropped and Matt started to realise that there was more to running an online business than a great idea and someone to build the website for you. Actually, it is no different to setting up a physical shop on your local High Street. You still have to gain credibility, entice passing trade and generate sales, as well as carry out bookkeeping tasks, engage in marketing activities to find people who aren't just passing by, create a creditable brand, logo and design for your business and products, and so on. Did I mention manage and pay employees, complete tax returns, deal with returns, set up possible partnerships with other shops next door, spend time talking to people who like your products but have no intention of buying or who look at your products and buy something similar but cheaper in the next town?

My brother's idea was great, but the problem was that he thought it was the product alone that contained the most value. In reality it is the entire set of business assets which add value to a product. From choosing the company name and creating your first logo design right through to making your first sale and beyond – three, five and seven years down the road – plus every conceivable task you need to carry out in between. The product itself is only 1 or 2% of the business model, unless you are incredibly lucky.

My brother's story isn't too unfamiliar in my daily life, either. My primary role within my business is business development and sales, and while I don't profess to be a business consultant I have seen a great many businesses. From businesses which are just ideas right through to well established international companies. I've got a well-honed gut feeling for what works and what doesn't work.

Online businesses always achieve startup status. However, many experience a 'failure to launch'. These failures occur because of a lack of one or more of the following:

- Core Business Model/Framework
- Resources (People, Time, Money)
- Marketing Strategy

In order for an online startup to launch, be successful and stay successful through the wilderness years, you have to be willing to fully commit to all three areas of your business. I hate to say it but it's also about the right time and right place: without a little bit of luck in such a competitive online marketplace, having the right foundations in place will only get you so far, but if you do everything properly you stand a much better chance of standing out.

This book is written for those just starting out on the adventure of setting up a new online startup and to those web developers who may be looking to gain an edge on their competition. I did not want to write another *Dummies Guide*; let's face it, you are not a dummy. This book is written for the serious entrepreneur who has considered or is considering creating an online business. I've written it as if I am talking to you, personally, in the way I consult with a new customer in a 'discovery session'.

I hope you will find some useful nuggets in this book which has developed from my practical business knowledge. This sits neatly alongside my expertise in helping all of my customers experience growth and scale within their organisation. The book is divided into four parts: preparing your business; getting online successfully; reviewing your website; and finally, marketing your business through social media.

There are a number of tips as well as some simple exercises which I encourage you to carry out. Towards the end, a number of tools are introduced, such as the Site Launch Checklist, which I use daily to audit customers' websites and ensure they are as good as they can be.

While I have tried to avoid being technical; some of the more common problems that affect a website's performance are identified and may require a website professional to help you resolve them. Or simply give your web developer a copy of this book once you have finished reading it, as it will highlight a few tools that may be useful to them too.

PART ONE
STRATEGY

What I wish I had known 10 years ago

STEP 1

Choosing Your Company Name and Registering Your Business

This is one of the most important decisions you will have to make in the life of your business. The company name will identify your business for the foreseeable future. It is possible to change your company name, but doing so could have major implications – particularly as your business becomes more established. You will have to go through a re-branding process which could be costly; you may have to create a new logo, brand and colour scheme as well as printed materials, website re-design and any intangible costs such as the confusion it might cause amongst your customers.

Therefore it is really critical to get it right now.

There are three main options when it comes to deciding on a company name. Firstly, you could use your own name as your company name. This is absolutely fine, but it may be tougher to present yourself professionally as a brand. This does however work well for Authors, Freelancers, Sole Traders or Professional Speakers, where it is about the person.

You could choose to name your company based around your products or services; ABC Plumbing and Heating, for example, which describes what it does but isn't necessarily creative. However, this sort of company name may help in search engine rankings because it has your main product or service within it.

The final approach is all about building a brand so it stands on its own two feet. Major companies these days are all about brand identity: Google, Apple, BMW, Audi, Yahoo!, Samsung, Coca Cola, Visa, Starbucks, Adidas, McDonalds and so on. They are all brands that people readily recognise; the idea being that once people remember your unique brand name you will be found in the search engines, and if it's catchy it will stick in people's minds.

Think about how your company name will look, maybe as a part of a logo or on your website. It shouldn't be too long and may have a bearing on what usernames you use for marketing your business on social media platforms. You will also be registering a domain name, setting up a website and having emails linked to the domain in due course, so picking a company name that can be reflected in your website domain name will also help. You can double check both of these by:

1   Googling your chosen company name(s) to see if anyone is already trading using those names
2   Check with a domain registrar, such as Fasthosts (http://www.fasthosts.co.uk/domain-names/), to see if your preferred domain name is available

It goes without saying that it needs to be unique. You can check if your chosen name or something similar has been registered with Companies House or Intellectual Property Office in the UK; or in the US, the Patent and Trademark's Office.

Consider how it will be perceived by your potential customers. It might be a great idea or quite funny at the time to give your company a catchy or clichéd name, however, you need to consider if, in a few months, it will continue to appeal to potential new clients.

You may choose to operate as a Sole Trader, Limited Company or Partnership when starting out. Registering as a Limited Company is my recommended route as it is a simple process and protects the Intellectual Property surrounding your company name. In the UK, the process of registering a Limited Company is straightforward. There are three options:

1 Find a reputable Chartered Accountant and ask them to register your new company on your behalf
2 Use one of the many Business Registration websites available
3 Do it yourself on the Companies House website – http://www.companieshouse.gov.uk

Registering the business directly through Companies House is probably the cheapest. However, an accountant will have experience in registering businesses and will understand what share structure you will need to set up from day one.

 TOP TIP

Do check on Companies House to see if a company name already exists. Equally, someone may have registered your chosen name as a Trademark, which means you can't use it as your company name. You can search registered trademarks on the Intellectual Property Office's website – http://www.ipo.gov.uk/

Using one of the third party websites to register a business also makes life slightly easier than the DIY option however, from personal experience, they make the process more complicated. They register the business on your behalf with themselves as the key shareholders and then transfer the shares into the name(s) of your company director(s). Director Shareholdings are recorded permanently and if, like me, you have OCD, it looks a bit messy on the paperwork.

I would probably feel comfortable registering a new company directly with Companies House now, but our accountant is great and takes all of the hassle and worry out of the process.

When registering a company in the UK, you only need one Director and a Company Secretary, who can be the same person.

Once registered you will get a Registered Company Number, and will be legally obliged to complete annual Company and Tax Returns on an annual basis. A good Chartered Accountant may charge in the region of £500 per year to complete the various returns but they will ensure these returns are accurate and hopefully save you enough tax (to cover their costs at least).

You may also want to become VAT registered; HMRC adjust the UK VAT threshold each year so check what that threshold is on the HRMC website, you can still be VAT registered if your turnover is less than the UK VAT threshold. Once registered you have to charge VAT to your customers and complete quarterly VAT returns but you can also claim back any VAT on your outgoings. If your business does not have many overheads and is under the threshold then you may want to avoid being VAT registered, likewise if you are selling directly to consumers (B2C) then not being VAT registered will save your customers 20%. However, if you do have higher overheads, and are selling your products or services to businesses (B2B) then you may want to consider VAT registration regardless of whether you have reached the threshold.

IN SUMMARY

1 Choose a company name which you will like in five years' time

2 Decide whether you are the brand or whether your business will be the brand

3 Register your company name officially

4 Consider registering for VAT; having a registered company and VAT registration does look professional

5 Choose and register your domain name. Secure your Social Media 'handles' at the same time

STEP 2

Logo Design, Branding and Colour Schemes

 TOP TIP

Do engage with a graphic designer to help you develop your logo, branding and colour schemes.

These will be the first elements of your business that your potential customers will see, and it does take a professional graphic designer to create something which is clean, usable and professional. This will be your identity. Your logo will be what your customers associate with your company name.

If you do not yet have an identity, I first encourage you to carry out two tasks:

1. Look at other logos and brands, and find half a dozen which you like. This is an easy task: go to Google, search for 'Logos' and then click on the 'Images' link just underneath the search box. You will be presented with thousands of logos.

2. Get a pencil and blank sheet of paper and sketch out a few ideas. Ok, so a graphic designer can take a creative brief and create concepts for you, but if you already have an idea it helps to try and get what's in your head across to your designer.

Things which do not constitute a good logo include:

- Using Word Art or Clip Art.
- Using elements of other company logos and calling them your own; there are potential copyright infringement issues with doing so, which could have legal implications.
- Looking too much like your competitors' logos.
- Trying to include too much in your logo, it should be simple.

By all means start the creative process using some tools; a pad and paper, Word, Publisher, Photoshop or whichever tool you prefer. Once you've sketched out your logo, hand it over to a professional Graphic Designer who can then create a series of concepts based on your ideas.

This does not have to be an expensive process. For example, a graphic design agency will try to include about six to twelve concepts in one batch of work, which may typically take between two and four hours. These concepts can then be shortlisted down to two or three, which are then refined before selecting the final chosen logo. This is charged at an hourly rate which is agreed between you and your graphic designer. This should result in a really clean and professional looking logo. Your logo should be provided to you in Vector Format – scalable without loss of quality – as well as High Resolution JPEG and Transparent PNG formats for you to start using wherever you wish.

One way of doing this is to create the logo in black and white first, and then invert the logo to white on black to see if it still works. Once the basic logo works in black and white you can then start to layer the colours on. This way you know that you have a logo which works in colour and grayscale as well as on a black, white or coloured background with the correct contrasts.

Your brand isn't just about a logo, it also includes:

- size of the logo
- your associated emblem (if you have one)
- fonts
- colour schemes
- printed and online media
- style of images and photographs
- your company's tag-line
- your tone of voice
- clothing

The KISS (Keep It Simple, Stupid) principle definitely apply to branding. The KISS principle states that most systems work best if they are kept simple rather than made complicated, so simplicity is the key objective in the design exercise. You don't want to appear bland and boring but at the other end of the spectrum you don't want a brand which is all colours of the rainbow, complicated or confusing. The branding exercise is not an exercise in entertaining your customers; it is about creating a professional and memorable appearance, which your customers will remember for the right reasons.

 TOP TIP

Avoid clichés; they might be amusing now but they will be cringe-worthy in a year or two's time and you will find yourself having to re-brand.

Be careful with colours as these will have a bearing on how your brand looks across all printed and online media. For example using colours without enough contrast may lead to accessibility issues on your website. Try to plan ahead and choose colours with some contrast that will work well across all media. That way you'll keep all of your advertising materials consistent and won't have to introduce new colours especially for the website.

Your colour scheme should only consist of up to four main complementary colours, which can include black and/or white. Any more than four starts to become confusing to the end user and may result in an inconsistent theme. Try and avoid gimmicks like using different colours for different areas of your business and/or website. This creates confusion and inconsistencies. It can be done, but your graphic designer will need to be very experienced and have a great eye.

It is common amongst larger organisations to invest in a set of brand guidelines; I've seen examples of brand guidelines running into hundreds of pages before. For a smaller company or a startup, brand guidelines are an invaluable asset to your business, and can be as short as two to four pages long. Brand guidelines typically include:

- Your logo
- Inversions of your logo:
  - Black and White
  - White on Black
  - Full Colour
- Coloured Backgrounds
- A colour palette including Pantone, CMYK and RGB references
- Logo (and Heading) Typeface
- App/Website Typeface
- A very brief note about the usage of each part of the brand

Aim to create a set of brand guidelines no longer than two sheets of A4 paper, to which you can refer whenever you are creating a new marketing asset, such as:

- Business Cards
- Email Signatures
- Headed Paper
- Envelopes
- Brochures
- Website

Your brand guidelines document will save you a huge amount of time in the long run, because whenever you need to create a new asset you won't have to hunt around for colour references, or different versions of your logo or your fonts. They are all contained within one simple-to-follow document which any designer will understand.

 TOP TIP

No matter where your brand is used, ensure that it is consistent across the board, as this ensures your assets are instantly recognisable as your own.

IN SUMMARY

1 Engage with a Graphic Designer
2 Do plenty of research
3 Avoid using clichés
4 Create a set of brand guidelines
5 Ensure your brand is used consistently

STEP 3

Accounting and Bookkeeping

TOP TIP

The first thing that you should do when you set up a new business is find a reliable and proficient chartered accountant. Someone who understands small businesses, limited companies and partnerships, VAT, payroll.

A good accountant is absolutely vital to any business. A good accountant will pay for themselves through efficient accounting methods, good advice and tax savings. If you think that you can do it yourself then think again; it's not as straightforward as totting up your receipts and invoices at the end of year and working out the difference.

Do not try to DIY with your accounts. By all means do the day-to-day bookkeeping but a good accountant is invaluable. Being slightly naive, when I began my business I made the mistake of not doing my research and going for the cheapest accountant I could find.

Midway through my second year in business, it transpired he had very little experience in working with small businesses, and so the company started to accrue fines and letters from Companies House and HMRC. With the little knowledge I gained from one of the modules on my degree in Business Management, which covered financial accounting, I spotted a number of errors with his submissions. I found a chartered accountant who specialised in businesses like mine, with whom I had played rugby. It was the best decision ever, and not one single fine or late filing penalty notice has been received since.

There is no harm in knowing a bit about some basic business accounting yourself, although my advice would be to ensure you understand basic terminology as opposed to knowing accounting inside and out. Areas you could seek to understand would be: profit and loss (P&L) and balance sheets, cash flow forecasts, how turnover is defined, the difference between gross profit and net profit, understanding overheads and direct expenses. These constitute benchmarks which determine how well your business is performing; it's useful to get a snapshot of how your business is doing on a month-on-month basis.

An understanding of basic business accounts will also be useful when it comes to writing your business plan, as this information is vital in conveying your business pitch to a bank or investor.

Remember – you are not an accountant so concentrate on your core competencies, which are selling and fulfilling your products and services. Even if you don't take on an accountant straightaway there are some processes that you can put into place from the word go to make your life that little bit easier; easier for you throughout the year, and easier for your accountant at your financial year end.

⏻ TOP TIP

If you are thinking of taking on employees, definitely find yourself a reliable chartered accountant. Paying people is easy; payroll accounting isn't quite so easy.

The second thing you should do is subscribe to or buy some bookkeeping software. QuickBooks and Sage Instant Accounts are standard desktop softwares and work well; as do Xero and Sage One, both cloud-based bookkeeping solutions and can reduce time spent on bookkeeping tasks. I have many clients who have experienced a time saving of up to 80% in switching from a manual (spreadsheet/word processor) based system to a professional bookkeeping solution.

Xero has a great facility for easily setting up and sending out recurring invoices. This is fantastic if your business' revenue model is based around monthly or annual subscriptions, because you can automate the process of sending out recurring invoices. Xero works with lots of third party applications, so you can use apps like http://www.elastic.io/ or https://zapier.com/ to automate the process of adding contacts from your CRM (in our case, Salesforce) into Xero. Xero automatically imports a data feed from your bank, making the reconciliation a five-minute-a-day job.

You can submit your VAT returns directly from Xero. You can also give your accountant access to your Xero account so s/he can login and get a snapshot of the business. That is the beauty of cloud in that you can access Xero from anywhere with an internet connection.

I would recommend Sage if you have a larger organisation with a dedicated in house accountant; they have their own cloud-based solution, called Sage One, which is probably on par with Xero although there are many cloud-based book keeping solutions to choose from; it's worth shopping around to find one you feel most comfortable using.

Be regimental about filing your paperwork throughout the year as this will save you, and your accountant, time when it comes round to completing your annual returns. If you can neatly organise your receipts and documents into one or more A4 lever arch files to hand over at the end of the year that is fine. Better still, scan and upload copies of the documents into Xero. The important documents you need to keep are:

- Sales invoices
- Purchase receipts
- Expenses (including receipts)
- VAT return reports
- Payroll reports
- Bank statements
- Any notifications from Companies House and HMRC

Your accountant can help you set up a filing system for your paperwork. Keep a copy of the login credentials for any government gateways or software associated with your accounts and give this to your accountant, as he may need access to certain portals in order to complete your returns.

Do not wait until your year end to organise your paperwork as you will be unlikely to remember what happened at the start of the year, or what particular bits of paper were for. It will take you a long time to sort through all of your paperwork to present to your accountant if you only do it once a year, so allow five or ten minutes per day to keep on top of your bookkeeping.

IN SUMMARY

1 Find a cloud-based bookkeeping application – they normally have thirty-day trials so take advantage of the trials and find an application that you are most comfortable using

2 Find a reputable and reliable chartered accountant; even if their rates are higher, they will save you money in the longer term

3 Implement a good filing system and be regimental about filing your paperwork

4 Allow five or ten minutes per day to carry out bookkeeping tasks

5 Don't DIY your end-of-year returns

STEP 4

Business Planning

Writing a business plan is one of the most essential actions to complete when setting up a business. 25% of business fail within their first year, of which 95% did not take the time to write a business plan.

Writing the business plan is something you will do after you have chosen your company name, and maybe even after you have completed your logo design and branding. It is definitely something you should do after choosing your accountant as you will find his or her help invaluable when you get to the financial forecasts at the end of the business plan. Being able to apply your company name and branding to your business plan is helpful as this is what will help to make it stand out and look professional.

Your business plan is designed to outline how your business will be structured and how you intend to run your business in the foreseeable future. You will be creating a document, to which you will refer regularly over the coming years, and which determines how your business is going to be run. It outlines the main aims, objectives and goals for the business and the strategy you will be employing in order to achieve those milestones.

 TOP TIP

This is a really crucial document. Don't be one of the 95% who don't bother to write a business plan, which is the first step towards failure.

Your business plan could be targeted at a number of different people, such as funding sources if you are looking for seed funding, a startup grant from local government or charitable trust or some kind of credit from your local bank. If you are not looking for funding for your business this is no reason to shy away from writing a business plan as you can be the target of your plan – the one at whom it is aimed. This document outlines how your business is going to be run for the foreseeable future including the goals you set yourself. You can look back on the document in a year to check whether you have succeeded in meeting your goals or perhaps how far off you are from your projections.

On a practical level it will help you identify times in your company's life when you have perhaps chosen to pivot your business and take it in another direction, at which point you will need to update your business plan.

First and foremost you will be setting the scene about what your business will actually be doing, as well as the authority that you have for setting it up in the first place. This is especially important if you are seeking funding, as investors will generally be looking to invest in the person behind the business as much as the business idea itself. You can have a fantastic idea but if the investor isn't confident you will be able to deliver the goods then they will be reluctant to invest. You need to have experience in the field of expertise surrounding your business' purpose and can hopefully demonstrate this through past employment, your education or another business venture, in which you have been involved.

Before you move on to shouting about the great idea or product you have developed, it is a worthwhile task to carry out some market research and display the results in the business plan. A great solution is only great if it is solving a legitimate problem, so you have to prove that there is a problem first before you begin to offer a solution. Your market research will have helped you identify your target market, which will lead into a marketing plan to outline how you are going to get your products or services in front of that target market.

The financial forecasts are the hardest part of a business plan to pull together as they require a realistic assessment of your anticipated revenue and costs. Anticipated doesn't mean 'hoped for' and needs to be realistically based on factual research and market intelligence. If you are looking for funding of any sort then the financial forecasts are critical. These will include profit and loss and cash flow forecasts for the first three years of the business, broken down month-by-month, plus a snapshot which shows the yearly totals on one page.

Nobody has a crystal ball so you are not expected to be able to predict how well your business is going to perform financially over the next three years so I have a number of tips which will help you to present a realistic plan, which will stand up to the scrutiny of your potential investor.

It still amazes me when entrepreneurs walk into my office and make me that offer, about which I had been dreaming for years;

'Hi I'm so-and-so and I've got a great idea, it's a mash-up of Facebook and Twitter but different and is going to be worth millions of pounds in three years, I'll give you 50% equity if you build it for free!' Wow, thanks, but I think I will pass on that one.

These types of ideas tend to have a modest revenue in years one and two, with a small net loss, and then miraculously by the end of year three they are turning over millions with an 80% gross profit. Most businesses will see some growth, it will be modest and tends to be linear. Create a revenue model with a growth of 25% year on year, where the net profit goes into the black midway through the second year after the startup costs have been paid off. Insane year-on-year increases in turnover look exactly that – insane.

Your accountant will come in very handy at this point as he will be able to spot any flaws in the figures you have created. He or she will have a better understanding of what is realistic because they are likely to have dealt with a great number of different types of business and be able to see what is common in your industry. If you have just engaged a new accountant then this is a good opportunity to see how they work, so perhaps ask them to help you with your profit and loss and cash flow forecasts for your business plan. Provided you have done the donkey work, it may only take them a few hours to complete the forecasts for you but it's a great opportunity to see how they work.

The attention to detail at this stage is important, which is also why an accountant is helpful. A potential investor is going to be scrutinising your figures to make sure they add up; an accountant will make sure that everything is in the right box and moved from one year end to the start of the new financial year. Banks work in numbers so they may turn straight to your financial forecasts to see if they add up.

Look at other examples of business plans for inspiration. Some further research about your competitors and their routes to market. This will help to identify any direct barriers to entry, for example if one of your competitors is already well established in your local area it might be tough to break into the market. What better way to conduct your research than hearing directly from other businesses within your chosen industry. Look at the common ideas, concepts and forecasts within other business plans as this may provide some direction for your own plan.

You can buy market research documents so this is a good means of ascertaining the viability of your business within your chosen industry. Sometimes doing some simple maths is enough to analyse whether your business idea is actually viable or not.

Divide a sheet of paper into two columns:

In the left hand column write down your revenue model for a month. This is as simple as a projection of where your sales will come from. i.e. your research has told you that you can sell 1,000 widgets at £10 each, therefore your turnover is £10,000.

In the right hand column write down all of the items which make up direct expenses (costs directly linked with the manufacturer of a product or delivery of a service):

- Cost of raw materials
- Outsourcing
- Overheads (indirect variable costs which enable the day-to-day running of a business):
- Rent
- Warehousing
- Marketing
- Salaries
- Telephone and broadband
- Postage and packing
- Accountancy fees

- Subscriptions
- Insurance
- Staff training
- Travel
- IT software and consumables

If your direct costs and overheads tally up to £8,000 then you have made a Net Profit of £2,000 or 20%.

 TOP TIP

A saying which has always stuck with me, 'Turnover is vanity, profit is sanity.' A business turning over £100k a year but creating a net profit of £20k is much more successful than a business turning over £1m but only producing a net profit of £50k. The former has a net profit of 20% while the latter only has a net profit of 5%.

On the flip side, try to avoid painting too dim a view on your projections and forecasts. I have seen many business plans go to the extreme in an attempt to not over-egg their chances but no-one wants to invest in a business which never makes a profit. If your financial forecasts display lots of red then maybe you want to reconsider starting that business.

Your business plan may include an outline of its operations scaling up over a number of years, so this needs to be reflected in your direct expenses and overheads. If you are selling products which involve a factory for manufacturing and warehousing for storage of stock you will need to sell more products to increase your turnover. Selling more products may lead to a requirement for a bigger factory and warehouse so make sure your costs go up accordingly with your turnover. A service sector business may need more staff as their customer base increases. A hosting provider will need more servers as their hosting capacity is used up.

Building a business is not entirely based upon risk, or at least it shouldn't be as far as the business plan is concerned. Ensuring that your business scales realistically in your plan is important. Although it has happened to some lucky people, the chances of starting up a business and making it a worldwide success within the first year are slim. So maybe rein back your hopes and dreams for the business plan and go county or state wide in year one, national in year two and international in year three. Plus, where is the excitement if you do it all in the first year?

I have seen business plans which run into hundreds of pages, and have bored me absolutely senseless. You don't want it to be too brief as you may leave out some vital pieces of the jigsaw however if possible, keep your business plan to approximately twenty or thirty pages of well-structured content. Some businesses may require more detail, but in my experience a business by nature should be a simple concept. You may be pitching to people who do not know the technical aspects of your field, so keep the language simple and avoid jargon where possible.

IN SUMMARY

1 Write a business plan; yes, definitely write a business plan
2 Carry out plenty of market and desk-based research
3 Provide realistic financial forecasts and ask your accountant to double check them for you
4 Keep the business plan succinct; twenty or thirty pages of well-structured content is adequate
5 'Design' your business plan and apply your new company branding to it

STEP 5

A Website without a Business Model or Strategy

Strategy

ˈstratɪdʒi/

noun

1. a plan of action designed to achieve a long-term or overall aim. 'time to develop a coherent economic strategy'

The website is not the business, it is merely an extension of the business. Therefore a business must have a strategy in place which can then be applied to the website. With a business you still need to be cautious when going through the website design and building processes; as with anything, a lack of planning often leads to failure. A common misconception is that a website is going to transform someone's business from a semi-successful one into a multi-million pound behemoth within the first year.

Many organisations also think that the website is going to be a cheap means of gaining extra sales leads without any of the usual overheads. For a retail outlet the website is a bit like opening up another showroom to a wider audience, from where you will be serving your customers virtually rather than physically. You will still need extra resources to manage orders and update the website on an ongoing basis. This shop doesn't close, it is open 24/7.

In your business plan you will have identified your aims, objectives and goals and then explained how you are going to achieve those through marketing, financial and business strategies. This must be reflected in your website so that everything is consistent. Failing to adhere to a consistent strategy will mean that you have to manage two different areas of the business, which will make the management of your organisation harder. Strategies try to address the uncertainties which make it difficult to predict how your business and website are likely to evolve and change over time. Many new startups want their website to be all singing and dancing with every feature under the sun before they have answered the simple question, 'How are we going to deliver this?'

Your business plan should be able to answer this question, as it will map out the deliverables and hopefully how the business will scale and grow. If you have planned a phased approach to growing your business then this should be reflected within the website's evolution.

Applying a phased approach to managing your website is a good way of managing your overall strategy, as it tends to lead to tasks happening in the right order ensuring that your business is scalable. You have already started on the journey of creating a business by choosing a company name and developing your brand identity. You know what your business is about and have identified your goals in your business plan.

The first step of a phased approach is to create a 'holding page' for your company. A holding page is a single page which says who you are, what you do and shows the end user how they can contact you to make an enquiry. Is it a coincidence that your business is quite young and you've only just worked out who you are and what you do through the branding and business planning stages? You can use a holding page to announce to your potential customers a time-line of when your products are going to be released, or when your book is going to be published or when your services will be available. It scratches the itch to get something online; it then creates thinking time for you so you can start thinking about, 'What Happens Next?'

 TOP TIP

Google operates on a trust basis, with one of those trust metrics being the age of your domain and the earliest point at which you published some content on that domain. Getting a holding page up on day one means you have gained several weeks or months of trust before your main website goes online.

New businesses often try to run before they can even walk. They have a wonderful idea about a new product they want to sell and so they want an ecommerce website now. What they need to do first is test their market thoroughly.

 TOP TIP

Test your online market first before committing to building a full ecommerce website.

CASE STUDY: Before my client launched a new software product I helped them to create a micro-site explaining what they were doing, and added a Demo Sign-Up form. They spent a finite amount of money on a targeted Pay-Per-Click campaign and within 30 days got an insight into their potential target market. The feedback my client received told us that people didn't want to pay for this product, but might be willing to contribute to the source code as an Open Source product. It was invaluable. My client was about to invest £50k in software development. This caused them to pivot and take a different, less costly, path.

There is a common misconception about building your own website that if you have a basic understanding of IT you are capable of creating an online presence yourself. I might be able to go out and buy some wood and basic tools and create something which resembles a chair but I doubt it would last long if you sat on it. You might be able to create a website which achieves some interest, say ten enquiries or product sales per month. Ask yourself this question: 'How would I feel if I only increased my overheads by 20% but increased my enquiries or sales to fifty per month?' A 500% increase in enquiries for a 20% increase in costs. This may seem implausible but it can happen if you choose the right organisations, with which to partner.

This could be the difference between engaging an online marketing agency, an SEO expert or having someone build you a well organised, standards compliant website. It is vital to build an outsourcing strategy for work in which you are not an expert. Once you have found an accountant, it is a good time to look for a competent web design agency or online marketing agency. Even if you can't afford it straight away, plan for it in the future when your business starts to grow.

The average life cycle of a website is two to three years. This is often ignored; we have customers who come to us having never updated their website in ten years. Our customers' strategies may not have changed much as their target market and niche may still be the same. However, the methods of delivering their website will have changed significantly, especially with the advent of 'mobile first': the number of people browsing the web using a mobile device is growing all the time.

Businesses that are not geared for change, do not to plan ahead or save or invest in updates to their website on a regular basis, will experience a sharp decline in visitors and enquiries. Google changes its algorithm so often now that, combined with the speed of change of modern technology, you can be sitting at the top of Google one day and be nowhere the next.

The business model you use to service your client needs to be consistent with your website. How you handle offline enquiries must be reflected on your website, so that your customers get a consistent message. Ensure your response time for online enquiries is equal to your quick response time for telephone calls. If your offline target market is not the same as your online target customers, you end up having to implement two different systems to manage customers with different expectations. It is important to align your sales channels with how you deliver your products or services to your customers.

During the discovery sessions I hold with my customers I will always talk about their business first. This enables me to make an informed recommendation on what is the best solution for the problem they are trying to solve, instead of getting bogged down by a list of features they want to see on the website. This approach allows me to refine the feature list later to a core set of features which will enable them to meet the goals they have laid out for their customers. Sometimes it highlights problems with our customer's strategy. Too many products, too much choice, a complicated pricing structure, too many shipping options, not enough choice, too wide a target audience or niche.

Sometimes business owners themselves are the main problem with the business strategy.

CASE STUDY 1: I recently had a discovery session with Sue and Emily, a mother and daughter partnership running a successful flower shop. The Session lasted ninety minutes. We spent thirty minutes talking about the website. They then spent fifty minutes of the meeting discussing which of their core products was the most important to promote on the website. I find it interesting to watch how business partners interact with each other as I get an overview of where each partner sits within the business. Before the conversation spiralled into an argument, I spent ten minutes drilling into the financials and helped them to identify six seasonal products to run special offers on in each of the four seasons, as well as Christmas and Valentine's Day.

CASE STUDY 2: David and Mark, a father and son team, had divided opinions over where their business was going. David had developed their websites over the past ten years as a hobby which then turned into a business, but he now wanted to retire. Mark wanted to work with a local company and hand over the responsibility of the websites to an agency, but David was reluctant because he was emotionally attached to the existing website. Diplomacy was at its highest during that meeting because it was no longer about the website at all. In order for that business to move forward, David had to retire and hand control of the website over to Mark. We settled on testing the water with one of their websites, which went very successfully. David is now enjoying the cruise he always dreamed of, and Mark has the independence he needs to take the business forward.

These sorts of problems are ones which affect the core of the business, and need to be ironed out before you go through the process of creating a new website or updating your existing website.

A simple question I ask is: 'What do you want your customers to do when they view your website?' It is surprising how many reply with answers along the lines of; 'You're the web designer, isn't that your job?' or simply, 'I don't know.' If you can't answer that question yourself then it's time to take a step back and look at your business plan.

A website is about getting someone from Point A (normally the website homepage) to Point B (completing a goal such as buying a product or making an enquiry) in as short a time as possible and with as few mouse clicks as possible. A website is your online sales patter and is different to how you conduct your business offline. Done correctly it can process the sales for you: it can take payment on your behalf, then send a note to the warehouse, where someone else can dispatch your products. All while you sleep in the middle of the night. It can even send monthly reminders about special offers automatically, prompting customers to come back. It can update your bookkeeping package automatically with today's sales and take money automatically for recurring subscriptions. All while you take a holiday somewhere nice.

IN SUMMARY

1. Get your idea online and early
2. Test your market with a proof-of-concept or minimum viable product
3. Phase the steps of increasing your online presence
4. Set realistic goals and expectations
5. Be prepared for change; the online world changes quickly

STEP 6

Aims, Objectives and Goal Setting

An aim is an intangible or tangible intention or aspiration. Objectives have measurable outcomes and are stepping stones on the way to meeting your aim. Goals are short term achievements which make up each objective.

George T Doran introduced the SMART criteria for Objectives in the November 1981 issue of Management Review, whereby objectives should be S.M.A.R.T.:

- **Specific** – plan ahead and be precise about your next steps
- **Measurable** – how you measure when you have reached a goal
- **Achievable** – set achievable goals and objectives
- **Realistic** – is the goal attainable given your resources (time, money & manpower)
- **Time Constrained** – set a deadline by which to achieve your goals

Many new business owners get swept up with the excitement of setting up their own business and often forget why they are actually doing it in the first place. The motivation for many of whom are leaving a job to startup their own business is to have the freedom to work for oneself. Now take a step back, in a job you were earning a regular salary, so one would expect to earn the same salary under the remit of your own business. In this example the aim is freedom, not the objective. The objective here is to generate enough sales to create profit and provide you with a regular income.

Within your business plan you will have outlined a number of aims and objectives for your organisation culminating in a series of financial forecasts. The most common mistake is to focus on the top-line; the turnover. I have made this mistake in several business plans, and I have several friends and customers who have made similar mistakes.

⏻ TOP TIP

Decide on your main objective and then work backwards. For example, if you want to earn £40k per year, add on 20% to that for tax, add on the overheads for the year, and add on your direct expenses and this will give you your targeted turnover (or your main objective). If that number is £120k and you sell your widgets for £1,000 each, your objective is to sell 120 widgets that year and your goal is to sell ten widgets this month. Your aim here might be to be able to give away one widget per month to charity. This is an aspiration which comes off the back of successfully achieving your longer term objectives.

Objectives determine what challenges you are going to face within your business for the period of time you have decided. This may start to raise questions like, 'How will I find ten new customers per month?' 'How can I up-sell my customers to two widgets?' 'Can I manufacture ten widgets per month?' If you are unable to make ten widgets per month then you are not going to be able to sell ten widgets per month, which makes your objectives unrealistic. This is a good juncture to pivot and focus on your manufacturing bottleneck and resolve that as a short term goal.

CASE STUDY: In practical terms, I helped a client to set out the following goals, objectives and aims for their graphic design business:

- Goals – To complete 10 projects per month
- Objective – To achieve a portfolio of 200 customers
- Aim – Once they have achieved 200 customers they want to give away at least one project to non-profits for free per month

By helping charities, they fulfil what they want to achieve for their own corporate social responsibility, however their financial position will not enable them to do this, and do it well, until their business is cash flow rich. For me, that is an indicator that they have achieved their objectives and now they can start giving back.

Within the corporate structure I have developed my own personal aims. I want every business I work with to be great, and to help business owners grow their businesses through great design, by using emerging web technologies and adhering to standards compliance. Their customers will have a fantastic user experience. I don't just want this for my own customers either; I am advocating that every web designer, freelancer and business owner has access to my knowledge to build great websites themselves.

 TOP TIP

Don't just think long term objectives; think final term objectives.

I see a lot of small businesses living in the now, and the near future and not further ahead into the future when perhaps it is either time to move on or retire. I still have the drive and passion to come into work on a daily basis and do what I do. Will I still feel the same in another ten years? I don't know. So, another objective that my partner and I are building into the business is to create financial security now as well as looking beyond the lifespan of our company.

For small business owners on a modest income it may be difficult to picture early retirement with a comfortable income, or to have enough saved up to live on for a number of years.

For a long time I felt that an exit strategy was somewhat defeatist. I've now realised that I cannot do what I do forever and selling a business needs to be a legitimate objective. A long term strategy should therefore revolve around having a business which could be sold if you so wished.

The graphic design company I mentioned earlier had a revenue model which was based on unsustainable project fees. They had created a business with no value. Even if they had wanted to sell it had no value. By pivoting their strategy and turning their key objective from project fees to monthly retainer packages for a number of VIP customers they have now created a business with a modest saleable value based on a monthly recurring revenue stream.

There is nothing wrong with having a ten year objective to sell the business. If you are an entrepreneur then this will appeal to you. I like the idea that there is a possibility that in ten years any one of my clients could have exited their business with a pot of cash looking for a new startup opportunity. Better still, I hope to get my clients' businesses into a place whereby they are working well within their own right and it provides the owner with some free time to look into other ventures.

The same rules at the start of this chapter, for working out your monthly income, also apply to working out your ideal exit fee.

TOP TIP

If the magic number is £1m, what Turnover and Net Profit will you have to reach by year ten to achieve this and what framework will you have in place to ensure this turnover is repeatable?

One element, upon which I haven't yet touched, is ensuring that your goals and objectives are measurable over a period of time. A simple way to measure the success of your website is to add Google Analytics. Within Google Analytics you can view unique visitors over a set period of time and also create specific Goal Conversions. A Conversion is when someone completes a pre-defined action on your website such as completing the checkout or submitting an enquiry form.

Within each Conversion you can also create a funnel of activity. For example, the number of visitors who:

1 Landed on the home page,
2 Clicked on a product,
3 Added it to their basket and
4 Checked out.

The funnel allows you to see visually how many people achieve each stage of the funnel and where people drop out. If you see a large percentage of people dropping out between adding a product and checking out then you can begin to analyse why they might not be completing the checkout process. You can modify the checkout and hopefully then increase the percentage of people checking out and be one step closer to achieving your sales goals for the month.

Auditing, reviewing, testing and making changes are fundamental parts of realising your objectives. If you are not achieving your objectives you can implement changes to move you closer to your objectives. Setting arbitrary objectives and not double checking that you are achieving them is a total waste of time. There are plenty of free tools available like Google Analytics to audit the progress your business is making (see Part 4 – Review, Step 4)

Failure to meet simple objectives, especially conversions on a website, may highlight issues on your website, about which you are blissfully unaware, or perhaps illustrate that your customers are interacting with your website in an unexpected manner. For example, if Google Analytics has identified several email form submissions have been sent successfully but you haven't received an email notification then these could be lost sales. Conversions on a website is entirely a numbers game, and it is better to have auditing processes in place on a number of levels. For the typical contact form we ensure there are three means of measuring enquiries:

1   Conversion tracking via Google Analytics
2   An emailed copy of the form submission
3   The details submitted are added into the database, and a notification appears next time you log into the CMS control panel

With three means of measuring conversions in place there is no way that a sales enquiry can be missed.

IN SUMMARY

1 Remember to be SMART
2 Work backwards from your main objective
3 Consider your exit strategy
4 Determine what value Turnover and Net Profit you want by year ten
5 Audit, review and test thoroughly

STEP 7

Proposals and Deadlines

The only way to achieve goals is to set deadlines; a goal is irrelevant if it can't be measured over time.

Projects are made up of a number of components and steps, all of which are, or should be, measurable. At the start of a project, if our customers have a specific deadline in mind, I will look at a calendar and work backwards through it building in the various steps and phases of a project until we get back to the start.

Sometimes deadlines are just unachievable. If you realise that the deadlines are unachievable at the start of the project my best advice is to start negotiating then. Waiting until part way through the project to negotiate over deadlines creates a psychological barrier between you and your clients. It creates a level of distrust, 'Why is the deadline now this date? You said it was going to be launched on that date! That's the date I've been giving my customers and now I've got to tell them something different! I'm going to look unprofessional!' By setting realistic deadlines you will be doing you and your customers a favour. A common mistake is to be coerced into bringing a deadline forward for a customer. This is of cardinal importance if the deadline is missed; the finger will solely point at you.

When proposing either very large projects, or where the customer is likely to change scope part way through a project, it is sensible to introduce a buffer. Changes of scope occur when the customer's expectations change part way through a project. Always produce a proposal ahead of your projects which the customer can sign. Within a proposal you can outline estimated start dates, the duration of the development of the project and an estimated completion date. Build a buffer into that, and those dates are moveable. If the project starts a week late then the deadline is also shifted by a week. If there is a change in scope of the project (i.e. additional features on top of what was proposed to your customer) then this will push the deadline back by the amount of extra development time required. If the customer's deadline is an immovable object and the feature is required then it incurs an extra charge in order to cover the extra resources required to build it.

I like to think that I am creating partnerships with my customers and that I am not merely a supplier. A proposal, with agreed (but estimated) deadlines, is a good middle ground because it means that there is a contract between both parties.

If a customer questions a deadline it is helpful to draw their attention back to the agreed deadline and remind them that, 'We agreed that this project would take eight weeks to build and now you want it built in six' or 'We agreed 120 hours on this project before June 8th however the extra feature is forty hours additional work, we just don't have the time to deliver that.' A proposal presents clear outcomes within pre-specified timescales.

Likewise, get any changes of scope in writing to ensure absolute clarity. Your customers already come to you with pre-conceived ideas about how much your products or services will cost and what sort of company yours is. It is however your responsibility to manage your customer's expectations and needs from the outset.

CASE STUDY: A large holding company with about a dozen brands engaged James, a freelance web designer. It would have been a mega contract with, potentially, a new website build for each brand. He went through his sales pitch over the telephone. After the call James completed their new supplier forms, and dutifully sent them back. He arranged a follow up meeting and set off on the three hour trip to meet the customer.

The MD totally ignored James when he walked into their meeting room despite being introduced to him. The meeting lasted for two hours. It actually went quite well; they even told James that it had gone well. However, an hour into the three hour drive home he received a telephone call from the Marketing Manager:

'Hi James, you did really well and we shortlisted two companies. We were split 50/50, however you didn't get the gig. Sorry!'

'Do you mind if I ask you why?' asked James.

'Because you are a freelancer, we only work with agencies of ten or more people!'

It was a really valuable lesson in customer expectations.

 TOP TIP

Regularly review the progress of your project.

Build in a series of 'scrum' meetings with customers throughout a project: at agreed points in development, hold a physical or Skype meeting to check they are happy with progress, then keep these regular and perhaps more frequent towards the end of the project. This means that you don't get to the end of the project and then discover that your customer is unhappy; you can uncover problems and react sooner, pivoting where necessary to bring the project under control. It is also a good opportunity to review progress against deadlines.

TOP TIP

Learn to say, 'No!' to your customers as easily as you learned to say, 'Yes' to them.

Negotiating deadlines is sometimes just about being able to say 'No!' to your customers. One of the best tools you can implement when negotiating deadlines with difficult clients is to quote the 'Get Real' triangle of Time, Quality and Cost. When push comes to shove you can only have two out of the three.

Time:

If you are short on time (e.g. by the customer bringing a deadline forward) you may compromise the quality of the project or the costs. This may be in terms of overall quality: given more time you could iron out all of the bugs and test your product thoroughly. It may mean lack of features; if the deadline is brought forward you just don't have the capacity to include all of the features your customers asked for. Costs may go up because in order to meet a new deadline you've got to increase capacity by bringing in more resources in order to meet that deadline. This means you can have:

- a project on time at a high quality but it impacts on costs, or
- your project delivered on time and on budget, but the quality may be sub-par.

Quality:

If the quality of the build of your project is not negotiable, then you will have to forego some time. So the project will take longer. Or you will have to negotiate on cost. A higher quality product will naturally cost your customers more money. You can only have:

- a high quality product, within budget which takes longer to build, or
- a high quality product which is built on time but will cost more.

Cost:

If budget is limited, then you will have to forfeit either the quality in terms of fewer features and functionality or you will have to expect the project to take longer to build as your developer may choose to prioritise better paying jobs ahead of your own.

There are very few small businesses out there who are able to deliver a high quality product, on time and on budget; many of them lack the capacity or expertise to be able to deliver all three.

What this means is that if you set yourself an unrealistic deadline then you have to be prepared to suffer the consequences. This could mean having to work late and at weekends when creating time is the only way to generate more capacity. Over-committing to deadlines puts you under additional pressure. There are many people who believe that deadlines are a means of, 'Getting things done!' This is true but deadlines should really be a guideline to the finish date, and it is not always possible for everything to come together the way it was anticipated.

I always ask myself the following question, 'Will someone's life depend on us meeting this deadline?' This may seem somewhat extreme to some of you, however invariably the answer is, 'No!'. So let's find a way of limiting the damage of failing to meet the deadline and find a way of moving towards our goal as quickly as we can. Deadlines can provide focus but from experience they do also create lots of anger and resentment if they are missed. It is your responsibility to your customers to understand whether the deadline is critical, for example if the website launch coincides with a product launch or exhibition the next day. You have to know what your customers want, and manage their expectations accordingly.

⏻ TOP TIP

If you are going to miss a deadline then let your customers know at the earliest possible opportunity. It may be bad news that you are delivering but your customers will appreciate your honesty in the long term and the heads up so they have time to react. There is nothing worse than reaching the final deadline to then be told it's not going to happen.

IN SUMMARY

1 Always provide time estimates in your proposals
2 Get a signed proposal – this forms the agreement between you and your customer
3 Regularly review the progress of your projects
4 Learn to say, 'No!' to your customers
5 Let your customers know, as soon as possible, if you are going to miss a deadline

STEP 8

Creating a Scalable Online Business

Creating a scalable business is not just about making your business ready for incremental growth; it is also about creating a commodity. You are in business for one reason primarily and that is to make money.

Creating a scalable business is about creating security. There are a number of key elements to creating a scalable business which will ensure that your business is generating a regular monthly income with minimal stress. Running a business should get easier as your business gets older, but in practice that is not the case. Don't be afraid to re-purpose your business and take it back to startup mode.

You can apply these principles to any business, so take a look at your business and ask yourself the question, 'Is my business scalable?'

Too many small businesses rely on one or more employees, most commonly the business owner(s) who are essential to the business. If they take a holiday the wheels start to fall off. As a business owner you need to make yourself redundant by ensuring that your role is teachable to others within your organisation. This can be done by documenting your methods and frameworks and teaching these to other members of staff. If you look around you will see that businesses like yours are everywhere, but it is the unique approach that you take which sets you apart from your competitors. Finding a core value, to which your competitors do not have access is the key to making sure you stand above your competitors. This core value will be based upon your knowledge and experience. Knowledge equals value.

Intellectual Property is created when you have created the frameworks and models within your business and ensured that these tasks are teachable, learnable and repeatable. If you reach a point where your products and services are repeatable then you can add in an extra layer to the model, which is to automate the process. 99% of small businesses rely on a core set of staff to deliver their products and services. If your costs and the number of staff required go up incrementally with the number of units you sell, this only creates complexity within an organisation. The more you can automate, the more profitable your business is going to become. This has been evidenced by the huge rise in the number of cloud based 'software as a service' businesses over the last two to three years. These services give you the option of simplifying and automating things like bookkeeping and accounting, warehousing and distribution, (social media) marketing, design, customer relations, email and ecommerce.

There are few businesses which are completely automated that don't experience an increase in overheads as they scale up. At worst you should be aiming for your gross profit percentage to remain the same as your business grows. Sometimes it is impossible not to incur capital costs, as you may require office space and warehousing as you expand your business into other countries for example. What you do want to avoid, where possible, is that the operating costs per unit do not start to creep up. With capital investment this may be unavoidable but the investments should create future economies of scale and reduce unit costs overall. Maybe if your company is not able to absorb capital expenditure but your business is scalable in other departments perhaps you could consider licensing or franchising your core products and services in order to facilitate the required growth.

⏻ TOP TIP

During growth there are two key areas:

1   Your existing customers – As businesses go through periods of growth existing customers can become forgotten and neglected. Ensure you have a process in place to monitor your existing customers and ensure that the service you provide to them does not decline.

2   Ability to deliver an increase in sales – Investing in a sales team or increasing productivity creates a chicken and egg scenario. Growth in a business means increasing unit sales. Ensure you have the ability to keep up with demand if you are expecting to go through a period of high growth.

One of the first things a potential investor may be looking to happen, is for you to leave. If you leaving makes everything grind to a halt then your business may not be a worthwhile investment in their eyes. So develop a business model which others can be taught and make the process repeatable. Having a team who all understand the core values of your business and how it works is essential to creating a scalable business. Your staff will likely be invested in their jobs, whereas you started your business because you are an entrepreneur who is looking for new opportunities. This could be new customers, or new investors.

Outsourcing non-essential services which can be carried out by anyone is essential, as this creates time for you which will be invaluable. You can use this time to change your focus onto activities such as marketing to grow your customer base. It will add additional value into your business which you can plough back in through product design and innovation.

Introducing the *lean* principles into your business will create an open ended business which strives for continual improvement.

This is achieved by introducing shorter feedback loop cycles. One cycle of the feedback loop is the length of time taken to release a version of your product to your customers. Instead, you create a series of Minimum Viable Products (MVPs) which you can put in front of your customers with shorter intervals between versions. Rather than waiting for feedback for six months and then pivoting, shortening the feedback loop cycles to a few days or weeks will save your business valuable time if it the change or new feature is something your customers don't want.

 TOP TIP

Regularly ask yourself, 'Is this product the right product?' This forces you to step into your customers' shoes, and look at your products objectively and determine whether it is the most appropriate solution.

Choosing the right marketplace is a priority. Likewise being able to pivot when you realise you are in the wrong market. It might be that within one market you could reach a saturation point quickly and when saturation is reached your business is no longer scalable because your potential sales pipeline will dry up. Therefore choosing the right market for your business is essential to ensure that your business will continue to attract customers for many years to come. This can be backed up by basing your strategic plans on choosing the most profitable market. The ideal target market will have a good mix of profitability and saturation levels; being able to demonstrate that this market has a long future ahead will also attract investors in the future.

If you are considering building your business to sell it in the future, then you could opt to find a suitable investor at an earlier stage. An investor with experience in your field may be able to transform your business. This also means that when you reach that difficult decision of letting the business go, you will already have an investor on board who knows your business well. This removes the fear factor from the process of selling, knowing that you will be leaving your business in good hands with someone who you know and trust. It also adds a level of excitement into the process. If someone perceives a value on your business at an earlier stage, this is a great compliment.

IN SUMMARY

1   Knowledge creates value; create a manual of your processes
2   As your business grows, don't forget about your existing customers
3   Invest in core personnel who can either deliver sales or your product
4   Ask yourself, 'Is this product the right product?'
5   Keep an eye on costs as your business scales

STEP 9

Marketing Strategy

At university I learned marketing theory, but much of it is barely relevant. Of the Four Ps that we were taught – Price, Product, Promotion and Place – only Promotion is still vital in the internet market. You need to be promoting yourself and your business all the time, everywhere and to as many people as you possibly can. The following key marketing tips can help you jump-start your business, and many of these tasks you can do yourself for free.

Make use of the many Google Applications which are available. Google accounts for 90%+ of search engine traffic these days, and Google has invested many billions of dollars in various apps which are free to the user. While they claim that allying yourself with Google's Apps has no bearing on the PageRank they give you, I have a sneaky suspicion that it does.

Google Maps and Google Places

When you carry out a search for your business type and location (e.g. Plumbers, Gloucestershire) a list of businesses will appear at the top of Google's listings and within their Maps App, Google Places. When you sign up for this they will send you a postcard with a pin number on it to verify your business premises, and then place a marker on the map. You can then create a profile for your business on there, including your address, telephone number, opening hours, short description about what you do and a link back to your website. All for free.

Google Plus

Google+ is Google's own Social Media Platform which allows you to create a business page similar to that of Facebook's and LinkedIn's Business Pages. In a similar fashion to Facebook, Twitter and LinkedIn you can create a detailed business profile linking back to your website. You can then fill that page with a number of links, status updates, photographs and videos all linked to your website, business or industry news. People add you into their 'circles' and 'follow' your page. You should also make use of the communities on Google+ as this is a good means of networking and having discussions with topics surrounding your business niche(s) which you can use to drive traffic back to your own website.

Online Reviews

There are many websites, including Google Places, where you can encourage your customers to leave positive reviews (hopefully) about your business. Obviously the more reviews you get then the higher up the Google Places (and other websites) you will appear. Generally site traffic is now governed by search, and so people will be steered towards whichever businesses feature prominently in whichever platform they are searching first. If you do not rate highly then you may never be found, so you don't even get the opportunity to sell to potential customers if they don't even find your website.

Offline Reviews

Your best form of marketing will be your existing customers. A good word-of-mouth referral will come to you as a pre-sold lead so milk it. Provide a good service to your existing customers and they will refer business your way. You can even massage good relationships with your customers by offering them a reward for the referral, such as a discount off their next order. Customer testimonials are invaluable; customers who have had a good buying experience will be happy to provide testimonials for you to use in your marketing material so never be afraid to ask for one, especially if you know your customer is a happy one. Use these testimonials on your website. You can also ask your customer if it is OK for you to create a case study about them to go alongside their testimonial. This is perfect because for potential new customers it sets the scene by telling a story, with which hopefully they have some affinity.

Online Portfolio

Create an online portfolio for whatever it is that you do. Your credentials are key to collecting new customers. Potential new customers will be looking at how long you have been in business, the types of customers with whom you normally work, and how many of them you have. Create an online portfolio of your best work and be prepared to share your best customers contact info with potential new customers.

Social Media Profiles

There are so many social media platforms available now that you can create profiles on hundreds of social media platforms (if you have the time) for free. The four main ones are Google+, Facebook, Twitter and LinkedIn, but sign up to as many as you feel are appropriate to your business. They normally allow you to add a number of details about your business including a link back to your website.

Update Social Media Regularly

Just having social media profiles is not enough, you need to be updating them on a regular basis. I would recommend posting status updates to the big four platforms (Twitter, LinkedIn, Google+ and Facebook) at least three times per day. You can use apps such as

SproutSocial, Buffer, Klout or HootSuite to schedule your posts. This means you can spend a morning once a month creating your social media content, and schedule it using one of the aforementioned apps and then forget about for the rest of the month. If you are struggling for content to post then you can look to create posts about the following topics:

- A daily featured customer
- Testimonials from clients
- New products
- Industry news (with your take on the article)
- Countdowns to product launches or workshops
- Upcoming events
- Photos
- Questions you would like answering
- Retweets, favourites and replies
- Quotes
- Top Tips
- Thank yous
- Connecting other people

Blog Regularly

This is probably one of the hardest tasks to get into the habit of doing, and it also contains one of the biggest misconceptions. People still think that blog articles should be long white papers that no-one is going to read. You can blog about any of the items that I've mentioned above, and it only has to be two to five paragraphs as long as you ensure that it consists of well-worded and well-optimised content.

Ultimately what you want to do through blogging and updating your social media content is to encourage visitors to visit your website and hopefully start to engage with you there before buying your products or services. Which is why I tend to post content which is mostly linking back to our own websites and products.

Share Your Expertise

There are many places where you can share your expertise with people. Including your blog, forums, social media and many other places. If you present yourself as an expert in your field or market, then potential customers will be drawn to you. Often those who choose the DIY approach will gravitate to an expert when they need professional help that relates to whatever subject matter you are posting. Likewise, by providing your expertise in this manner you are demonstrating honesty, which is likely to encourage potential customers to refer you or use your services.

 TOP TIP

Never ever shy away from giving your knowledge away for free. It is your biggest asset and normally leads to people asking you to facilitate your expertise. If someone tries to copy your methods or business model they will never be able to do as good a job as you can. Have confidence in your products and services. You need to own your market as well as your unique selling point and stand for something big. Customers will gravitate towards you because you have a bigger vision than those who are copying you.

Run regular workshops and take part in local networking events so that you can meet people and tell them about what you do. Be an evangelist for your own products and services. Share your expertise on a series of YouTube videos, not least because this is another Google product which will boost your organic search engine ranking. YouTube is the second most popular search engine after Google… and it's owned by Google, so exploit it!

Free Gifts

One of the best means of attracting new customers is to offer them free gifts. We are not talking about pens or bags with your own branding on it, but something which is actually useful. This could be a PDF download on your website with a list of Top Ten Mistakes You Commonly See in Your Industry or Top Ten Ways to Improve Your Widgets. Do not collect *anything* in exchange for this. Find some information you can give to your customers entirely for free.

Corporate Social Responsibility

Do something good for charity or the environment. I am not suggesting for one second that you do this because you have to for marketing purposes, but I hope that most business owners have a sense of purpose within them to help others and the world around them. Pick something which is close to your heart and support it. Your passion for your cause will come through in the way you run your business on a day-to-day basis and will appeal to your customers.

Pay-Per-Click and Paid for Advertising

Pay-per-click (PPC) advertising is exactly as it says. In short it is a method of advertising which means that every time someone clicks on your advert, normally linking to your website, you pay the advertiser a small fee on a per-click basis. The two most common advertisers around at the moment are Google Adwords and Facebook Ads. Google Adwords works on a bidding mechanism, so that you bid up to a maximum fee per click against other businesses. Someone bidding more than you will appear higher in the 'Sponsored Listing' section on Google. Facebook Ads is slightly different. While they do offer the traditional PPC model, they also offer a pay-per-impressions model. This means you are bidding between £0.04 and £0.10 for every 1,000 times your advert is displayed. This is independent of the number of times your advert is clicked on.

PPC is a good way of bolstering your advertising when the chips are down or you are having a slow period. However there are two very important words of caution:

If the PPC campaign is not managed correctly costs can quickly spiral out of control. Or you can spend your budget very quickly and receive few clicks. Many people have a bad experience and spend money quickly and never try it again. A well optimised PPC campaign which is constantly reviewed can be very beneficial.

If you end up relying solely on PPC then beware. When times are hard, and you have to cut back your marketing budget this will have a direct impact on the number of enquiries you will receive. I have seen several instances whereby customers have been spending solely on PPC as opposed to their organic listings in the search engines. Organic SEO is where you try to improve your rankings within the organic (non-paid-for) listings within Google. When they switch off their PPC campaign, their site traffic plummets because they are not appearing in the organic listings.

Retargeting

Retargeting is a form of online marketing which targets consumers based on the previous websites which they have visited. In particular where they have visited your website and it hasn't resulted in a sale of a product or a website enquiry. A pixel or cookie is placed on the user's web browser and then ads are served to them as they browse other websites linking back to your website hoping to re-engage them in the future.

 TOP TIP

Engage with a leading Marketing or PR Agency in your local area who specialises in your chosen niche. They will have a huge amount more experience in marketing than you will. But do continue to follow the tips above as, done correctly, this will only help with your online profile. Also, traditional forms of marketing do differ from online marketing so there is nothing wrong with engaging someone who specialises on Digital Marketing to work alongside a traditional marketer if they complement one another.

IN SUMMARY

1 Use the many free web applications available to you; be prepared to pay for those that you really value

2 Ensure your profile and business pages are complete and reflect your brand

3 Create a portfolio and get testimonials

4 Share your knowledge wherever you can

5 Engage a leading marketing or PR agency who specialises in your niche

STEP 10

Strategy for Change

The one thing, for which businesses most forget to plan, is change. Change is the hardest piece of the jigsaw to predict, which makes it the hardest thing to include in a plan. Change is the most likely thing to affect a business moving forward and changes created by external forces are the hardest things, to which an organisation can react positively.

In the first eight years, I successfully grew my business to a six figure turnover based on project fees alone. This was fantastic while the projects were turning over. Alongside this I had a small business web-hosting package, which was only really a token payment to cover server fees and some management time. In 2012 the recession finally caught up with me: the projects were still coming but I was caught out in three areas.

Firstly, businesses dramatically cut their marketing budgets meaning project fees went down.

Secondly, the many redundancies generated by the recession created an increase in the number of web design freelancers, which created extra competition. I am happy with competition but, being set up as an agency when most new customers were making their decision purely based on price, the freelancers tended to be the only winners.

Finally, a silly mistake which I don't mind admitting. I hope that making this next point public knowledge will ensure that other organisations don't make the same mistake. I failed to give proper attention to the support and hosting contracts, meaning that when project fees dropped off so did the regular monthly income which was needed to support the ongoing costs and overheads.

A significant strategy change in the following years has created a balanced revenue model of monthly support fees and ongoing project fees, which has the effect of stabilising cash flow and creating additional value in the business should I ever want to sell. The value of a business includes guaranteed regular revenue from existing customers, and not just turnover alone.

To achieve the new structure and ensure our business model achieved change, we made several key changes within our core business:

Offloading time-consuming tasks

Along with our basic web hosting package we also used to include support for email hosting. Using our dedicated server we had the ability to support both, so we did. Ten years ago most of our customers only had a PC and maybe a laptop, so supporting email was easy. With the invention of Tablets, Smartphones and other mobile devices all of a sudden we were taking four times as many support calls and it was costing us money to support our customers' email solution. Given that our service has been about quality, we felt that we were no longer in a position to offer an Enterprise level email solution, so we found a suitable partner and went through a lengthy process of migrating all of our email hosting and support across to a new provider.

It was the best thing we ever did, our support calls went down by approximately 80% and it allowed us to focus on what we do best, which is design and deliver fantastic websites for our customers. Our top line wasn't affected and it reduced our overheads. Plus our customers now get a much better quality of dedicated support from our IT & Email partner.

Out with the old and in with the new

This next decision was really difficult. We had a number of very loyal, but not very active, customers, some of whom had been with us for several years and never committed to any further updates. This accounted for approximately 40% of our customer base. Our new business model is based upon active customer engagement through regular support and updates. It felt like putting a gun to some of their heads as these were people who we enjoyed working with. We provided lots of notice and throughout the process they were given the choice of coming on board with our new strategy or moving to another partner (who used to work for us).

75% chose to move – mostly basing their decision on ongoing costs; but 25% stayed and upgraded.

It is difficult to express just how tough it was to make this decision, but it now means we do not have to support any legacy customers, and the current customers fall neatly into a specific niche. I want to help as many people as possible, but I also believe that time should be honoured by a fair payment. When clients start to haggle with you over prices, features and your hourly rate then that is a good time to review the relationships with your current customers. No matter how much you like your customers, if they are a drain on resources or starting to hold up the growth of your business then there is nothing wrong with cutting them loose; provided, of course, that you handle the migration process diplomatically and, as was the case with several of our customers, work with them to find a new provider.

Complex projects vs simple projects

The one light-bulb moment I had during this process was in regards to our focus on project costs. On several occasions, we had been advised to shoot for bigger customers and bigger projects, but this seemed to bring more complications. Historically we have only ever charged a single fee for Support and Hosting which was £50 per month per customer regardless of the scale of their project. We were trying to manage a small number of large ticket projects. These were often complex, customised web-based applications, which then required lots of ongoing support. When I looked back and analysed the projects over a period of three years I noticed some alarming figures.

We had spent a period of time before and during the start of the recession focussing on a number of £10k plus projects, which only generated one £50/month support and hosting account per project. The light bulb moment was realising that for each £10k project we could potentially have developed 10 x £1k simple brochure style websites each of which could have generated a £50/month support and hosting account.

The answer was simple; we pivoted to focus on smaller businesses and improved our Service Level Agreement (SLA) geared for Support and Hosting. We also introduced a new policy for charging a percentage of project costs (5%) as a monthly support fee on larger projects over £1k.

The unpredictable vs predictable changes

What the new charging structure allowed us to do was focus on improving the technology we use to host and serve the websites we provide to our customers. The monthly revenue is what we re-invest back into the business to constantly evolve and improve our core products. When Microsoft chose to deprecate one of the programming languages, which we had frequently used to build our customers' websites, we had the capital to invest in migrating to a new programming language with very little significant impact on our existing customers. When their website's life cycle was up and they wanted to upgrade we had a simple upgrade path onto the new platform and most were none the wiser.

Having a regular monthly income with a focus on the customer allows us to make changes within our business.

We were forced into making some of these changes, not all. You will face changes in your business which you can predict and others which you cannot predict.

 TOP TIP

Always be willing to adapt to changes when they occur, whether or not they were predicted.

IN SUMMARY

- Don't create a kneejerk reaction to change
- Offload time-consuming tasks
- Keep projects simple
- Change is not always predictable
- Be willing to adapt to changes when (not if) they happen

PART TWO
WEBSITE

**Common problems in
developing websites**

STEP 1

How to Find Great Web Design Agency

 TOP TIP

Do not base your choice of web design agency solely on price. Cheap means that you are not doing your website justice.

A good web designer or developer will have a standard day rate which is equivalent to any other professional organisation. The starting point is to cast your preconceived ideas aside and don't start the process of finding a new web design agency with a fixed budget in mind. Be open minded and try to compare several web design agencies based on their credentials and accreditations and not solely on how much they are going to charge you.

The price difference between the cheapest and most expensive may not be that much, however the product and end result from the most expensive agency might be phenomenally better than the cheapest.

You need to have a clear idea in your mind about your expectations from your web design agency and you ought also to shop around, as you would with the purchase of any product for your business. Approach three or four local design agencies for a quote. You can't beat being able to drop in to see your web designer, point at the screen and watch them make changes to your website right in front of you. If there is nobody local who is up to scratch, then you have the global marketplace at your fingertips and can always contact them with a Skype or similar video call.

I like to try and meet prospective customers at least once before anyone signs a contract, even if they are further afield. It is beneficial to me as I can learn a bit more about our customers, but it is more beneficial for our potential customer as it gives them some confidence in us as an organisation. They can see how we work, and to whom they will be talking when they call us. Business is all about creating partnerships and is much more enjoyable when you can work with people you like. Meet your potential web designer before you enter into any form of contract, as it is much easier to cut ties before you start working on a project, than at later stages if things are starting to fall apart.

Before you engage a web design agency and request a quote, it is helpful for them to have a specification document to quote against. On many occasions I have had people call and ask, 'I want you to build me a website, how much is it going to cost?' to which my reply is normally, 'OK, tell me a bit more about your business.'

Why do I look at the business first? It's purely down to looking at identifying the problem the website is trying to solve and to be able to offer up the best solution for that problem. Your specification document should outline the problem you are trying to solve through your website, and a list of features that you would like to include on the website. I can then gauge your expectations, and begin to advise which of those features are important...and maybe flag some additional features for you to consider.

Examples of features include:

- Newsletter signup form
- Contact form
- Location map
- Latest News / Blog
- Twitter Feed
- Slideshow on the homepage
- eCommerce
- Social media icons

It doesn't have to be a work of art, just a simple bullet point list of features. Encourage your web designer to be proactive too, by asking them what features they feel should be included in the website. They should respond with some positive suggestions for you.

From a design perspective, research the sites you like and don't like. Create a shortlist of half a dozen sites or themes/templates which you really like and present these to your web designer in your brief.

Also include in the brief, your logo and some branding so they know what style of design you already have in place.

Email this specification document to four or five web design agencies or freelancers. This is a great test too! If you email several agencies and they take a long time to reply or don't reply at all well that starts to whittle down your choices. Either the contact form on their website isn't working, or they're pretty useless at communication in which case, longer term, they might struggle to service your requirements.

I try to get back to new enquiries within the same or next working day. Sometimes it's not possible to get back with a detailed answer, so I will send a reply acknowledging their enquiry and request a good date/time for me to call them.

If the prospective design agency replies quickly via email with an immediate, and not terribly detailed quote, there is also a fair chance they will not understand your business or your requirements. That is why I will always have a discovery session over the phone or in person to really get to know the customer and iron out any flaws in their creative brief.

When you receive your quotations and proposal back from your web designers, ensure you compare the quotes that are like-for-like in terms of features and offering. Don't take it on face value that each quote is going to result in the same end product and don't select on price alone.

Talking of price, building a website is normally broken down into two parts:

1   The up-front costs of building the site
2   The ongoing support and maintenance costs

It is typical in our industry to charge a 25-50% deposit before any work is committed, but do ask for their terms and conditions up front. A contract protects both you as a customer and also the web developer.

For an enterprise solution I would expect charges to be along the following lines:

- £500-£1,000 for a simple brochure style site based on a theme or template

- £2,000 for a custom/bespoke design
- £3,000+ for a custom/bespoke design plus ecommerce functionality

For ongoing costs this may be a monthly fee in the region of £10-£50/month for support, web hosting, license fees and SSL certificates (if required). Plus a pre-agreed hourly fee for maintenance which might range anywhere between £35/hr up to £100/hr.

Look for answers to the following questions:

1   What does your 'package' include?
2   Where will my website be hosted?
3   How to do you handle standards compliance, accessibility, responsiveness and cross-browser compatibility?
4   How Search Engine friendly will my website be?
5   What support packages are available to me?

There are different sorts of web designers out there too. The two main types you will find are Freelancers and Agencies. Pick a web designer who fits the profile of your business. If you are a freelancer yourself then maybe a freelancer reflects your business better. If you need access to more resources then perhaps an agency would be a better option.

Above all, unless they have the right credentials, *do not* get suckered into having a website built by your mate's brother's aunt's son's daughter. A well-established freelancer or agency will have plenty of websites in their portfolio.

Likewise, unless you have absolutely no budget available at all, avoid the home hacks, DIY, free and build-your-own, solutions. In the longer term, these will be more harmful and costly for your organisation. These solutions do not allow your website to scale and grow with your business.

Returning to that earlier point, a website designer should be well established and have a portfolio of websites they have built. Be cautious if they have only been around for a few months or only have three or four sites in their portfolio. Unfortunately web design agencies and freelancers tend to come and go, and when they go it will cause you problems.

Perhaps when you have shortlisted one or two agencies or freelancers call up a couple of the customers in their portfolio and ask for a testimonial from them. A good web designer will have absolutely no problem with you doing this, so be wary of those who do.

IN SUMMARY

1 Create a specification document
2 Do shop around
3 Look for an agency or freelancer which:
   - is well established
   - you like and will get on with
   - has depth to their portfolio
4 Look at the level of detail in their proposal; have they outlined up-front and ongoing costs clearly? Compare proposals like-for-like; don't be tempted just to choose just on price
5 Get testimonials from their current customers
6 And once you've found a great web design agency, stick with them!

STEP 2

Be Realistic about your Feature Set

 TOP TIPS

when choosing the correct feature set for your website:

- Make a bulleted list of the features you would like to have on your website
- Ask your web design agency what is included within their solution for you
- Listen to your web designer when he or she gives you advice on which features you should have and the ones your should avoid
- Phase your feature rollout

Must haves vs nice to haves

A must have is something which your website must have in order for your customers to complete the end goal which you have laid out for them, and they must be able to achieve this as quickly and easily as possible.

Nice-to-haves will not necessarily improve the customer journey however they may make the experience of visiting your website more memorable and add to its stickability; how long someone spends browsing your website.

Nice-to-haves can be a bit gimmicky and if there are too many or they are overdone you can either put someone off visiting your website; confuse them so much that they leave without completing your goals; or just get distracted and forget why they are looking at your website in the first place.

The key to unlocking the feature set on your website is to *put your customer first*. Get into the mind-set of your customer and imagine what they will need to see on your website in order to follow the path you will be laying out for them. The easiest way to achieve conversions is to remove as many clicks and distractions as possible.

What is included?

It is rare these days to find a static website, which contains no elements of dynamic content (although we did just build one for a client recently as they wanted to be totally server independent). Static websites are very simple, basic HTML driven websites, probably limited to one or a few pages of content.

Once your website has been designed or you have chosen a theme it is more common for your website to be driven by one of the many Content Management Systems (CMS) available.

Most CMS platforms include a minimum level of expected features and functionality and it is worthwhile checking with your web designer as to which CMS platform they will be using and what features are available to you within their chosen CMS.

⏻ TOP TIP

Later in the book there is a chapter specifically about the differences between CMS platforms, however you should leave it down to your web developer to choose the CMS platform they are most comfortable supporting. You should not enter into the pitch phase demanding they use a specific CMS.

As a rule of thumb your CMS package should include the following:

1   Ability to add, edit and delete pages of content – goes without saying.

2   There should be some basic access levels and content moderation available. This means that Content Editors might be able to add content, but it will require an Administrator to publish the changes.

3   A latest news or blog plugin so that you can easily publish news articles on your website. You should be able to categorise, tag and archive blog articles and moderate any comments left against your blog articles.

4   A basic contact page including a space to edit contact details, a contact form and maybe a Google Map if you want your customers to visit you.

5   Social Media Integration – including links to your Social Media Profiles, as well as the ability for users to 'share', 'like' and '+1' your web pages.

6   Some element of ecommerce so that you can add, edit and delete product categories and products, add them to a shopping cart and then a checkout which is linked to PayPal, SagePay or WorldPay as a bare minimum.

7 Ability to add Google Analytics

8 A 'Rich Text' or What You See Is What You Get (WYSIWYG) Editor

What you should avoid

The critical things to avoid where possible are:

- Horizontal Scrolling – Most users are familiar with vertical scrolling now, especially on mobile devices and with the scroll-wheel on a mouse this is much easier. Horizontal scrolling is a pain.
- Carousels – Once upon a time they were all the rage, but it was a fad which didn't last long and now they are considered an accessibility nightmare.
- Complicated Animations – These can be a huge distraction, can be clichéd, often go against accessibility guidelines, and if your website still contains a Flash animation you are alienating a huge part of your potential audience (Flash does not work on Apple devices).
- Counter intuitive navigation – most people look for a navigation bar somewhere near the top of the page in a simple text-based format. Hiding your home page navigation (menu) in a complicated series of graphics, animated slides or at the bottom of your page will confuse users.
- Popups – Popup 'Can I help you?' or 'Sign-Up Here!' banners are just plain annoying.
- Splash Pages – These are intro pages before the user can access the main content of your website. It's just an extra click and may not convey the correct message, so avoid at all costs.
- Browser Hijacking – Disabling the Right-Click and slowing down the vertical scroll rate is incredibly irritating and creates

a poor user experience because it is making the web browser act abnormally to your site visitors.

Above all, get into your customers' mind-set. How can you get from A to B in as few clicks as possible and complete your goal? If your business is about serving information, products or services to your customers do you want to waste your money and their time by building fancy features to entertain them, or do you want to get the information they require in front of them by the quickest and simplest means available?

Consider how much time you are going to have available for updating your website once it has been launched. Adding in lots of extra features may require regular, time–intensive, content updates, which you hadn't anticipated. If you don't have a great deal of time available to update your website then consider looking at a set of features, which match your goals, aims and objectives and will also render the website self-sufficient.

A good example is adding a Twitter (or other social media platform) feed to your website. However if you don't Tweet on a regular basis then your customers will see a feature which isn't regularly updated, which may reflect badly on your commitment to your own business.

If you ask for extra features on your website, be prepared to commit time to updating the content for those features regularly; whether that's a social media feed, news blog, portfolio, testimonials or list of products. If you do not, the information on your website will quickly appear out of date. This is about creating a presence online which represents the core values, philosophies and virtues of your business.

Phased approach to releasing features

If your requirements are very complicated then there are several good reasons for breaking your project up into several manageable phases:

1   Firstly, it will make the overall project more manageable.
2   It is easier to make more accurate time and cost estimates for smaller chunks of work.
3   This will in turn make deadlines more achievable and finite.
4   If this is a new website your brand and website may not have immediate traction; an eCommerce website may incur higher monthly fees but if you don't have many site visitors, with which to start off, and therefore aren't going to sell enough products to cover costs, maybe you should focus on getting visitors to your website first and then switch on eCommerce during a later phase, saving you some money while you grow your audience.

Being realistic about what features you want to launch your website with is critical to its success. A full eCommerce website, based on a custom or bespoke design, with slideshows, animations, a complex custom CRM system and order processing system is going to take three or four times as long to build, test, debug and launch than a simple Brochure Style Website or even a Holding Page.

Search Engine Algorithms are all based on an element of 'Trust'. What this means in regards to your website domain is that Google will be ranking your domain's trust level based on the age of your domain. Not only that, but it will be ranking your website's trust level based on the first day you added content to your website.

Therefore it makes sense to get a Holding Page set up under your domain with the minimum amount of content to keep the search engines happy at the earliest possible stage. If you wait for six months to launch your wonder-app until it is absolutely 100% picture perfect you are already six months behind the curve in terms of gaining Google's trust. Therefore I would aim for the following three stages of deployment at the very least:

1 Holding Page
2 Brochure Style Website
3 ecommerce, plus bells and whistles

Eric Reis in *The Lean Startup* explains in more detail about the lean principles of launching a new product or application online. He talks about creating a 'Minimum Viable Product' or MVP which allows you to test your product or service on your customer base before launching the full product into the world. This MVP is improved through the 'Feedback Loop' and possible 'Pivots'.

The Feedback Loop Cycle is the process of adding a feature to your website in its simplest form, getting feedback from your customers at the earliest possible stage and then either implementing improvements or pivoting altogether based on the feedback you receive.

So, with a website, could you get your message out there through a Holding Page or Brochure Style website within say two to three weeks to start the feedback loop? If at this stage the feedback is negative, you can pivot. However, if you wait for your master app to be delivered which might take six months, you've committed an awful lot of time and money, to then receive negative feedback. Within this time you could have made several pivots or positive improvements to your app by speeding up the feedback loop cycle.

⏻ TOP TIP

Extra features generally add cost to your website build. Even if your chosen CMS platform includes a module that is ready to do what you want, the extra pages will nevertheless require styling to match the rest of your branding and colour schemes. If you are asking for lots of features then try not to be surprised if the quotations that come back are higher than you anticipated. If the quotations are too high then be willing to negotiate on the feature set to bring it within budget. Don't expect to have a custom, enterprise level, ecommerce website built for £200. Or at least lower your expectations as it may not be great.

IN SUMMARY

1 Choose your CMS platform carefully
2 Avoid adding annoying or clichéd features to your website
3 If your website is a large project, break it up into phases of work
4 If you are unsure of your market then first create a minimum viable version and get some real-time feedback before committing to the whole project
5 Extra features add extra cost to your website

STEP 3

How Much Does a Website Cost?

The real answer is that a website will cost you anything, from nothing (if you are happy with a hosted WordPress site, or a DIY website with the likes of 1and1 or Wix) to hundreds of millions of pounds, as demonstrated by the UK government on several occasions. The HMRC website cost £35 million per year to build and maintain for three years. Likewise the Business Link website cost around £105 million, including: £6.2 million on strategy and planning, £4.4 million on design and build, £4.7 million on hosting and infrastructure, £15.3 million on content provision and £4.5 million on testing and evaluation. These costs were repeated every year for three years.

A more pertinent question is, 'How much does a *good* website cost?'

Before you start to think about creating your new website you will need to purchase a domain name. You can do this yourself or, if you are thinking of using a freelancer or agency, ask them, who they would recommend you register your chosen domain with. There are several criteria I recommend for choosing a domain registrar:

- Their technical support is fast, responsive and helpful
- The control panel is easy to understand and simple to use
- They have no hidden fees should you try to leave

Registering a domain yourself will cost approximately £10 per year for a .com domain name or £5 per year for a local domain (e.g. .co.uk).

⏻ TOP TIP

One of the most common support requests that we get comes from customers who manage their own domain names and whose credit cards have expired or they forgot to tick the 'auto-renew' check-box on their domain control panel and then wonder why their website has stopped working. So, either pay your web designer to manage domain billing for you or remember to perform a regular health check on your domain.

⏻ TOP TIP

Don't register every domain suffix under the sun. Unless you are planning on setting up multiple different micro-sites (I cover this in the Marketing section later on), there is no benefit to having multiple domains pointing at one website. At the very most I recommend buying the .com and the .co.uk to our customers if they are available.

Costs will vary between freelancers and agencies, and depend on how you approach design and which framework you choose to build your website on. At a rough level of hourly rates: a freelancer will charge in the region of £25 to £50 per hour; an agency may be more like £60 to £100 per hour. However, both will offer fixed price project work for larger projects such as brochure style websites or ecommerce websites.

The marketplace for web designers is so competitive these days that you need to shop around to find a good quality designer. Remember, it is also an unregulated industry so shopping around will also help distinguish the good from the bad; the ugly tend to be obvious. As with anything, you get what you pay for and if it seems too good to be true then it most likely is. If a web designer is working too cheaply you will suffer one of three problems:

1   the quality of the website will be compromised
2   the length of time to design and develop the website becomes extended
3   the web designer becomes frustrated with the client because they feel undervalued (that's not the client's fault, though, it is because the designer didn't give a realistic quote)

Get quotes from multiple web designers, and question whether the cheapest quotes include the same set of features as the more expensive quotes; and look at their experience. A developer with more experience may be able to design and develop a website which packs much more of a punch that an agency with little or no experience. The websites we build now are light years ahead of the websites we were building when we first started out. OK, so the playing field has changed somewhat, but it has taken ten years to hone our skill-set and also know what emerging web trends and technologies to adopt or avoid.

If you have some technical ability then it is possible to set up your own hosting space with a WordPress website or other DIY website editor. There are plenty of really smart themes and templates to wrap your WordPress website in so that what presents is a professional looking brochure style website. The choice of plugins is good, so you can also make it feature rich. How good the quality is will depend on how far reaching your technical ability goes and at some point you will require the support of a website professional who has experience in developing and fine-tuning more complex websites.

This is a bitter pill to swallow though, as you managed to get your basic website set up for free but now you are going to have to pay someone to help you with it. That equals, 'No longer free!' It may just require a few tweaks, an hour or two of a WordPress guru's time. You will come to rely on your web developer eventually, so maybe commit earlier and save yourself the hassle later.

⏻ TOP TIP

For a typical brochure site build there is no harm in asking for a quote up front to ensure that this is a fixed price proposal.

Once your website is up and running then you will also have to pay for hosting, maintenance and support.

If an agency or freelancer isn't making a healthy income out of monthly support and hosting they may not be around for long. In the recent recession several local agencies fell by the wayside as project income ran out.

You will have to pay for an SSL Certificate on top of your normal monthly fees if you have an ecommerce website. You can buy an SSL certificate yourself but it is a complex process to install the new certificate. So as part of our package we take care of renewing and installing SSL Certificates on an annual basis.

⏻ TOP TIP

Ask for a fixed price quote up front for any ad hoc updates if you have a standard brochure style website so that you know exactly how much you will be billed for the updates in advance.

If you do go down the free or cheap route, when your business starts to grow your website will need scaling. When this happens be prepared to find a freelancer or agency and ask for some help. Be willing to pay for the privilege.

IN SUMMARY

1   Set your domain to auto-renew, and remember to update your credit card information. If your domain expires so does your website

2   Get several quotes, based on a like-for-like specification

3   Free and DIY do not equate to enterprise level websites, so be willing to pay for professional help

4   Most web design agencies will provide fixed price quotations up front for project work

5   Expect ongoing support, hosting and maintenance fees once your website is up and running

STEP 4

Bespoke Design vs Great Themes / Templates

Every web design agency has a slightly different approach to how they handle both the design and implementation of a website. From a design perspective it can be incredibly subjective, and if you are less worried about the overall look and feel there can be a great deal of choice available to you for the aesthetic design of your website.

A couple of years ago themes and templates were considered passé on the grounds that they all looked very samey, boring, nondescript and not terribly creative. Over the last year or two there has been a big revolution in terms of the style of themes which are now available to wrap up your website.

Up until two or three years ago you could really get away with just having a website; now there are specific design trends creeping into the web design industry so it is important to keep up with those latest trends. Luckily these design trends have filtered through into the themes and templates which are available and there are some fantastically professional, clean and creative themes available, for which you can buy a licence for a few dollars or pounds. Ensuring that your website keeps up with the latest design trends, means that it will be as future-proofed and timeless as you can make it.

One of the greatest driving forces behind the design trends, however, actually lies with the emerging web technologies and the CMS frameworks available at the time. For example, with the increasing use of connected mobile devices, responsiveness is critical on your website. This has led to frameworks such as Twitter Bootstrap, 1140 CSS Grid, Foundation, Boilerplate and Skeleton gaining in popularity. As a consequence Responsiveness triggered a raft of Responsive Integrated Designs.

Also, as Web Browsers develop slowly there is much greater control over embedding custom fonts into a website, created curved corners and drop shadows. Slideshows can be more creative and images dynamically resized within the browser to fit. This provides a huge increase in flexibility when it comes to design.

There are three forms of design typically available to you, these are:

A custom / bespoke design

The traditional form of website design used to involve a more complicated journey of creating a wireframe – a sketch or blueprint of your website – then mocking up the web pages by hand using Photoshop, Illustrator or the designers visual editor of choice, presenting the design visual back to their customer in a flat format (JPEG or PDF) for the customer to then approve or request revisions.

The main benefits of having a custom design created for your new website are that it will reflect your brand really well and contain a layout of the features you agreed during the proposal phase. It can be revised and agreed before being signed off. Your designer may also choose to offer optional layouts or styles, from which you can choose.

The disadvantages of going down the custom route are that it can be quite a time consuming process and often frustrating if your designer is having an off-day. It happens.

Even if a web design agency predominantly offers themes or the prototyping approach now they should always have the fall back of being able to offer a custom design service.

A theme or template

Themes offer the greatest choice in terms of look and feel of your future website. For example, a design agency might be able to mock-up three or four different layouts, from which you can choose, based on your brief and the allotted time. However there are thousands of themes available to you. My three favourite theme websites are:

* Wrap Bootstrap – http://www.wrapbootstrap.com
* Theme Forest – http://themeforest.net/
* W3 Layouts – http://w3layouts.com/

My advice when it comes to choosing a theme is to spend some time looking and to only go for a theme if you really feel it reflects your business well. Also, themes carry many different features within their layout so also ensure the theme you choose matches your feature set.

The biggest benefit of using a theme is that it removes the element of design required to create the layout of the website. When we might quote four days for a custom designed website this is usually made up of two days design and two days build. You can virtually halve the time and cost of getting your website up and running by choosing to use a theme.

The downside is that there is less flexibility in terms of getting 'exactly' what you want. However, I don't know many organisations nowadays that would not be suited to a theme, as themes are much more flexible than they used to be.

If you have a theme in mind, double check with your chosen web designer that she or he is happy to use that theme for your website; I would be surprised if they weren't happy.

Our customers' biggest concern tends to be that a theme isn't an original design, whereas in reality it is as good as an original. Some other website owners might be using the same theme but it is very unlikely that they are within the same location geographically or in direct competition.

A prototype

The final style of design comes in the form of a prototype 'hackathon'. The web design agency holds a two- or three-day workshop with the key decision makers within your business.

The customer is required to find half a dozen websites which they like the look and feel of, provide their brand assets, and finally choose a responsive 'bootstrap' theme which reflects their chosen layout. During the workshop your web designer will guide you through a creative process bringing together these assets to create a working prototype of your website. Changes can be made there and then to the look and feel until you are happy with the design and layout.

Once you have agreed and signed off on the prototype the web designer can then push straight on with the build and integrate the prototype into your chosen CMS platform.

Traditional web design involved creating wireframes, design visuals and numerous revisions which could sometimes take weeks. A design hackathon is high energy, exciting and involves the client in the creative process; most importantly it reduces the design process down to a matter of days.

TOP TIP

Remember the Seven Second Rule which states that within seven seconds of a user arriving on your website they must know:

- who you are
- what you do
- and where to go next.

Finally, ensure that who you are and what you do is clear through design and not just layout.

Many people get caught up in design, and what this can do is lead to a complicated layout which is difficult for your web developer to build. A complex layout could lead to complex HTML code, and it is the HTML code behind the layout, at which the web browsers and search engines look in order to carry out their jobs. Complex code could lead to standards compliance errors, broken accessibility, cross browser problems and worst of all make it difficult for search engines to index and crawl through your web pages. This is a disaster if this happens, because what is the point in having a great looking website if no-one knows how to find you?

It is easy to get carried away with fine tuning the look and feel of a website. I am a firm believer of the KISS principle when it comes to website design. Keep it simple at all costs; if the design starts to get too busy then your message will be lost when someone lands on your website.

IN SUMMARY

1 Website design is very subjective
2 Modern themes look modern and professional, but only use one if it reflects your core message or can be adapted to do so
3 Apply the Seven Second Rule to your home page (and any other landing pages)
4 Be careful when using faddy design techniques – flat design is already being superseded by hero images but responsiveness is here to stay
5 Remember the KISS principles – Keep it Simple

STEP 5

Don't Mention WordPress during the Pitch

If you are approaching a web agency, it makes sense not to say you want to use WordPress at the first meeting, even though it's been recommended or you've used it yourself. The pitch meeting is an opportunity for your web designer to understand the challenges your business is facing and to offer their solution to overcoming those challenges. Talking about technology too early in the process can sometimes distract you both away from the key business objectives and these challenges may be overlooked.

Don't get me wrong, WordPress does solve a number of issues; mainly budgetary and admin user experience. However, it lacks front end quality and customer user experience in many cases because it is improperly configured. The front end HTML code is where it all happens. This is the bit your customers see through their web browser and more importantly what the search engine's PageRank is based upon.

The important thing is that the HTML produced by your chosen CMS is Standards Compliant, meets accessibility guidelines and has all of the facets which keep search engines happy. Can you guarantee that a plugin created by a random programmer somewhere in the world has also been built to the same high standards? Probably not. Accessibility, Standards Compliance, SEO friendliness, Cross Browser and Device compatibility comes as standard within your chosen CMS platform.

I then have to spend the rest of the meeting trying to explain the difference between the many types of CMS platform available and that in reality any CMS will allow you to edit your content without being prohibitively expensive. It is down to the developer to choose the platform, with which they are most comfortable working. Ultimately they will have made an educated decision about which platform they feel will offer the most benefits to their end users.

⏻ TOP TIP

If all you want is a WordPress site and are unlikely to be swayed in any other direction, find a WordPress specialist.

If you like what a web design agency is doing and are open to other options, perhaps ask two important questions up front, 'My friend recommended WordPress; do you work with WordPress?' To which the answer might be, 'No'. So then ask, 'What are the benefits of your CMS over WordPress?'

I hope that the answer you receive will include some of the following:

- It is built using latest web technology XYZ
- Our CMS does everything WordPress does
- It is easier to use
- It is an Enterprise level CMS
- We can provide a better Service Level Agreement than we could with WordPress
- Our CMS is Standards Compliant, Accessible and honed for Search Engines

We have chosen to develop our own Open Source CMS for our customers because:

- It works on a server technology which we are familiar with
- It's written in a programming language, in which we are used to working (and is very popular; there are thousands of .Net programmers out there)
- It provides us with more flexibility, with which to customise websites
- We can fine-tune it to the nth degree in order to get the most out of it from an hosting and SEO perspective

WordPress is by far the most popular CMS framework available in the world today. It is now pre-packaged with many web hosting solutions so you can register a domain, install WordPress and away you go. WordPress is a great platform, it has a huge selection of plugins available which do a great many things.

It is great if you have a modest budget and want to set up your own website with one of the many thousands of themes and templates available. There are a huge number of really smart looking WordPress sites online.

In my opinion there are three very common problems faced by customers who currently have a WordPress website, and come to us because they want to move away from it.

1 There are thousands of plugins for WordPress, which is great news. The bad news is that they have been developed by a community of programmers ranging from amazing to awful. You could install a plugin onto your website, which either

conflicts with one or more other plugins or stops your WordPress site from working altogether.

2   From personal experience fine-tuning a WordPress site isn't an impossible task, but due to the community aspects of how it is built you cannot always guarantee that their coding methodologies are neat and easy to follow. Therefore customising and optimising someone else's plugin means reverse engineering their code first which isn't always a quick process.

3   Eventually all WordPress sites start to become boggy and slow down. Set aside a monthly budget to put towards optimising your WordPress website. WordPress was always designed as a blogging tool, never as a CMS, which is what it has morphed into.

With the three issues above eventually you will want WordPress to do something, of which it is not capable. Or hopefully your website is attracting so many visitors that it is crashing all the time. This is the time to start thinking bespoke, enterprise level and resilience.

Maintenance is difficult, and your developer may not always be able to accurately predict how long bugs might take to fix.

Migrating a WordPress website can also be tricky. We have partnered with a very experienced PHP developer who is an expert in WordPress – our 'go to' man for customers who are determined to have a WordPress website built – and I've seen several example of customers who want to transfer their hosting to another provider and their WordPress site simply won't work on the new platform.

Being able to set up your own website for free gives a false sense of security. When you do so and things start to go wrong, it can be a bitter pill to swallow when a developer tells you that you either need to re-purpose your website or that it is going to cost several hundred pounds to fix the issues with the current website.

What you want to avoid is having to pay for something twice whether it be in time or money. If you have grand visions for your website or business, starting out with a WordPress site may also hold you back because at some point you will have to redevelop your website on an enterprise level platform.

To give the DIY website route some credit though, it can be very helpful for a web design agency. A DIY website contains all of the elements of design, content, photos, structure and layout (hopefully) which you want on your website. Which saves us a huge amount of work. If you have some technical ability then go ahead and create your own website, when you want to turbo-charge your website don't be embarrassed to show it to a web designer and say, 'Look, this is where I am up to, now I need your help.'

We can see a clear picture of what's in your head already and it gives us a head start. Why not have a go at developing your own website first, and keep it in mind that there is a whole industry based on designing and building websites, we are here for a reason; because we know how to take good quality websites and make them great.

Later on in the book I will introduce several free(mium) tools which I use on a regular basis to test my customers' sites, and if you have built your own website I would recommend running these tests on your website to see how well it scores.

IN SUMMARY

1   If all you want is a WordPress site and are unlikely to be swayed in any other direction, find a WordPress specialist

2   There are alternatives to WordPress – let your web designer use their chosen platform to get the best results

3   Standards Compliance, Accessibility, Responsiveness, Usability, Search Engine Optimisation and Cross Browser Compatibility are all much more important than the framework used to deliver your website

4   Remember; WordPress is a supercharged blogging platform; it is not an Enterprise Level CMS platform

5   It is however a great DIY tool but find a good hosting solution to host your WordPress website – I would recommend a host that has a dedicated WordPress hosting solution

STEP 6

Finding Inspiration in Other Websites

Finding inspiration in other websites is all about short-cutting the creative process to help you fine tune what it is you like about other websites. Looking at the design, features, user interface and getting a taste for the user experience on other websites which will help you home in on the style of website that you would like to create for your own business.

During the early stages of a customer going through our pitch processes we ask them to produce half a dozen or so links to websites which they like the look and feel of. These websites do not have to be industry related websites, they can be any website which you like. From your local competitor right up to Apple or any large, well-known brands. The responsive framework we have chosen for our CMS is called Bootstrap and there are now lots of websites dedicated to themes and templates for Bootstrap such as:

- Wrap Bootstrap – https://wrapbootstrap.com/
- Theme Forest – http://themeforest.net/collections/2712342-bootstrap-templates
- W3 Layouts – http://w3layouts.com/

Theme and template websites are fantastic for gathering ideas because you have access to hundreds of different website themes and layouts within a single site resource. Who knows, you may even find a theme which you really like in which case you can avoid going through a lengthy custom design process with your web design agency and go straight to build.

Some customers try to create a list of websites which they don't like, but this isn't helpful in the creative process. It is much more helpful if we have a list of websites which you like because we can get inside your head and start to understand the concept you have for your new website. What is more helpful is a list of specific *features* which you don't like. This might be things like the CAPTCHA boxes on forms (the groups of numbers and letters you have to enter in order to submit a form), the use of specific fonts (e.g. Comic Sans), maybe you don't like big slideshows on the home page, or abstract photography in the slides, or the colour purple.

Alongside the six chosen websites which you like, also produce a list of a dozen features within those websites which you specifically like, for example:

- The Menu
- The Slideshow Graphic

- Call to Action Button
- Testimonials Section
- The Fonts
- The Colour scheme

Create a list of your most direct competitors; either those you are already aware of in your local area, or perhaps those you have found on Google, using keywords you would like your brand to be associated with. For example 'Tree Surgeons' – and then see who appears on the first page of the results. If your competitors already have great websites you can see how they have applied their design to their own website and what features appear on their websites. If there is a common theme running through the design and feature set on multiple websites, then perhaps these are features you should be considering for you own website.

Customers often come to me asking for 'something different' or 'to stand out from the crowd' but actually a great deal of psychology goes into the design and layout of a website…which is why the logo tends to be top-left, with a horizontal menu in the header and a hero shot underneath those in a slideshow with a big button saying 'click here' on it. Websites are quite similar because that is the layout which works best and with which your site visitors will be the most familiar. If you try to be too creative then you will confuse the user and create a poor experience of your website and ultimately your brand.

Creating extra features on your website just to be different is not acceptable; either it will cost you time and money and may not add to the customer's browsing experience. If you have a positive experience on a website or managed to complete a task quickly and easily on a website then take note, this is what the customer journey should feel like to your own customers.

⏻ TOP TIP

Always put your customer first when creating a concept for your website – you have seven seconds to tell them who you are and what you do. Your goal is to convert them into an enquiry, newsletter sign-up or a product sale as quickly as possible in as few clicks as possible.

Very few websites these days have an intro page before the main website. So why should yours? It is just an extra unnecessary click.

Here are a list of features on your competitors' websites, of which you should be taking notes:

- Logo, Colour Schemes and Branding
- The position and size of the logo on the page – there are two acceptable positions; either top left or centre aligned at the top of the page. Not top-right because it can easily be missed.
- Where the main navigation is – it is now generally acceptable to have a single horizontal navigation at the top of the page somewhere, but occasionally a site might have a second level vertical menu on the left hand side
- The slideshow (hero image), headlines and call-to-action buttons within the slideshow – is it full screen width or scaled to a fixed width? Slideshows also vary in format so try to find a format which you like and which reflects your business and brand
- Content layout, header formatting, fonts and colour schemes
- Newsletter sign-up form
- Footer formatting, link styles, colour schemes and position
- Social media icons – in the header, footer or both

- Social media feeds – e.g. Twitter feed
- Core services or featured products sections
- Latest news and link through to the blog
- Testimonials and featured clients

The more detail you go into at this stage the easier it is for your web designer to get a feel for the website which you desire. This creates the rationale behind a specific feature as you can qualify your feature request by saying, 'I want this feature, and I want it to look and work like this.'

As a rule of thumb, if there is a feature in your feature set (discussed in Part 2 Chapter 2) that doesn't appear on any of your competitors websites then ask yourself, 'Do I really need this?'

It is then the responsibility of your web designer to bring all of these ideas together into a single design visual or to make a prototype homepage, which will begin to form your own company's website.

Imagine if your specification was simply, 'I want you to build me a website.' compared with, 'I want you to build me a website; here are my brand guidelines. I love the Kickstarter website because the colours are clean and crisp and the main button really stands out because it's bright green. The login process is really simple, and the footer is really clean and consistent.' This is a much better creative brief to which the designer can work, but you will not be able to create that brief if you haven't first done the research.

The most difficult customers are the ones who, when we ask for this information, refuse to do the research and come back with, 'Well, you're the designer, isn't that your job?' Well, no actually it isn't. My job is to create a website which reflects your business and will help your business to grow. This is only possible if I fully understand your business, what your aims and objectives are and how you want to be best perceived by your customers.

Websites which do well generally tend to have a really consistent theme and message running throughout the entire website. Even if it's in the consistency of the design and layout itself. This might also be the style of images or use of fonts and colours; or the tone of voice which is used throughout the website's content. If you spot a consistent theme or message running through a website then definitely take note; an unsubtle consistent message will sell ten times more than a subtle gimmick introduced onto a website. You can ascertain whether a website's core message is unsubtle and consistent by asking yourself, 'Do I get what this website wants me to do?'

IN SUMMARY

1 Look at as many websites and themes as you possibly can
2 List half a dozen websites or themes which you really like
3 Make a list of at least a dozen specific features on those websites you like
4 Build your specification based upon those two lists
5 Ask yourself, 'What is the core message running through your website?'

STEP 7

I Thought You Would Write My Content For Me

In this chapter I want to demonstrate what your expectations should be in terms of what your website design agency will be doing for you. In very simplistic terms your agency is there to design and build a great website for you, and while they may offer other complimentary services surrounding the website it is best to establish and agree what these will be, as early in the project as possible.

Additional costs will be incurred for peripheral services such as:

- Copywriting
- Adding pages of content to your website
- Search engine optimisation
- Domain name registration
- Web hosting
- Email and IT support
- Social media management

We always agree to add between five and ten pages of content to our customers' websites. This helps us to test and ensure that the styling and content will be laid out correctly and enables us to give the website some substance before we demonstrate it to them.

However, we will not write copy for the entire website. This is the responsibility of the website owner because you (should) know your business and your potential customers better than anyone. I have helped to deliver over 200 websites over the last ten years, and I make it my business to get to know your business as well as I can through the partnership which we forge, but I can't get to know every business inside and out; especially the Unique Selling Points and the messages and sentiments that you want to convey to your customers about your products and services.

Therefore, it is better if this content comes directly from the horse's mouth. Your web designer will be able to give you hints and tips on how to structure your content for the website and may even be able to offer templates or video tutorials to aid you, but it is up to you to add the content and keep it up-to-date. Your web designer may choose to run through your copy once it has been added via your CMS to ensure that is it search engine friendly and error free.

 TOP TIP

Be prepared to add your own content, images and supporting documentation to your website.

If you really don't have the time to be writing lots of copy for your website then look into employing a dedicated web copywriter. There may be one within your chosen web agency, or you may have to find a freelancer. Do be prepared to pay for the privilege, this may be charged at an hourly rate, per page or at a fixed price agreed up front.

Your website will have a warranty period on it. The warranty period has two important deadlines associated with it:

1 When your web designer considers your website to be 'finished'
2 When your website finally launches

For billing purposes your web designer may choose to bill you when they consider their job to be complete. However, our customers quite often feel that they shouldn't be given the final bill until the site is launched.

The reason why we might bill when we feel the project is complete is down to the customer. This issue will mainly come up when they haven't finished uploading the copy and images for their website so it is not in a state of readiness to be launched. The web designer feels that she or he has completed their work, but if the customer takes two months to finish adding content then they could end up waiting three, four or even more months to get paid.

If the completion clause is written into the initial proposal and agreed by the customer then there can't be any argument. You can also agree a warranty period up front. Typically this is one month from the point that the website build is considered complete by your web developer. Within that warranty period, you as the customer must test your new website thoroughly, discuss any bugs, omissions and extras with your agency and agree a launch date. Then pay your bill within the terms stipulated. Launching a website takes up 0.05% of the time proposed to design and build a website and there is never an excuse for withholding payment because your website isn't live yet unless it has been pre-agreed with your chosen agency.

Once you are out of your warranty period, then you should have a support and hosting contract in place for your website. Your support contract should include a small amount of telephone/email support time for bugs and general help with managing your website. Ideally your web developer should not charge you for every tiny update they do to your website, but if they feel there is good reason to anticipate any significant update work, they should quote in advance to avoid any surprise bills!

Your web design agency will also provide you with some formal training in how to use their chosen CMS platform. We provide this training initially via a series of Video Tutorials which we have found has two benefits. First of all it means we no longer have to repeat the same training session for every new customer, so it saves us some time. We have found that nine out of ten of our customers find this provides an adequate introduction into the CMS to enable them to then go on and edit their site's content. Plus they always have the videos available to fall back on if they are struggling with an update or simply forget how to do something.

We also provide a second level of training via a telephone and screen-sharing conference where our support staff can walk you through the update, with which you are struggling. If it's a more complicated update that would be harder to grasp, but that we can do quickly ourselves, then it is quite often more efficient for us to take care of that update within the support contract at no additional cost.

The videos are available 24/7, telephone support may only be available during normal office hours. So, it is worth checking when and how support can be given. Most web design agencies work 9am to 5pm, Monday to Friday. Few agencies open at weekends, and even fewer are likely to provide support at weekends unless there is a critical failure of some kind.

TOP TIP

Your web agency is likely a specialist at designing and building great websites so don't always assume they will be great at everything involving computers.

We used to provide a much wider range of services but realised that we were in our sweet spot when designing, building, hosting and supporting brochure style websites. We used to offer IT and Email support, but technology has moved on so much that we had to find a niche and stick to it. However, the contact within your chosen agency will probably have a raft of partners, with whom they work, for things like IT/Email support, SEO, Online Marketing and Social Media Marketing. Always ask your web design agency who they would recommend first as it is highly likely they will know someone who can help. We always find partners who reflect our core company philosophies, ethos and working practices.

IN SUMMARY

1   Be prepared to add your own content, images and supporting documentation to your website

2   You are an expert in your own field so be prepared to write your own copy; and do so within a reasonable timeframe so your web designer isn't waiting endlessly

3   Ask about your website's 'Warranty Period'

4   Check what training and support is required once your website is up and running

5   Just because your web designer built your website it doesn't mean they are great at 'all things computer'

STEP 8

Setting Customer Expectations Post Launch

Whenever our customer's new website has gone live we always carry out our 'Site Launch Checklist' (which is outlined later in the book) which involves testing the site thoroughly and fixing any apparent problems with the website in its live environment. It is quite normal for some bugs to come out of the woodwork post launch, or for the site to behave slightly different between development and live environments. The good news is that any problems found at this stage are easy to isolate and fix and will be covered under warranty.

Two of the most important tools that we implement post-launch are:

1 Google Analytics – A free Google tool which monitors, analyses and reports your website usage
2 Google Webmaster Tools – Another free Google tool which monitors your website's presence within Google and notifies you if your website experiences any technical issues which might affect your search engine presence.

You may also choose to install Bing and Yahoo's webmaster tools for complete resilience, but we have found that if the site is being indexed correctly in the most widely used search engine (Google) then generally it will be indexed correctly in other search engines.

We run the website through a number of site validation tools including Nibbler, SortSite and GTMetrix to ensure the website and web server are running optimally.

If your new website is replacing an older website then we ensure that the pages indexed in the search engines redirect to the correct page on your new website, as sometimes the page URLs (web page addresses) might differ from old to new.

The full checklist is published later on in the book with instructions for you to follow so I won't go into too much detail now.

Your web hosting package should be backed up by a minimum Service Level Agreement (SLA) which ensures that your website uptime (how much time your website is available online) is as high has it can be. Your website will experience some downtime, even if it is only a matter of minutes per year. These periods of downtime will be due to security patches or software updates being applied to your server which may require your server to be rebooted. This normally only takes a matter of minutes to happen. An SLA is normally given in a series of nines, either three nines, four nines or five nines. For example a 99.9% uptime guarantee means that your website will be up for 99.9% of the time. This equates to the following planned downtime:

Availability %	Downtime / Year	Downtime / Month	Downtime / Day
99.9%	8.76 hrs	43.8 minutes	10.1 minutes
99.99%	52.56 minutes	4.32 minutes	1.01 minutes
99.999%	5.26 minutes	25.9 seconds	6.05 seconds

So, if you try to look at your website and it happens to be offline, try refreshing it in five minutes time as it is likely to just involve a server reboot. For anything more critical you should expect your web design agency to be on hand and working to fix the server issues as a priority above anything else, including at the weekend.

If an exceptional period of downtime occurs then your web designer should be understanding if you choose to move to another provider as a result, and they should be willing to offer a refund of your hosting fees for any lengthy period of downtime. However some downtime can be expected, and your website designer will not be liable for any losses incurred as a result of the downtime unless you have an upfront agreement with them that states otherwise.

Cloud based hosting solutions generally offer the best form of resilience. Cloud hosting is the term referred to a model of network computing where a website runs on connected servers rather than a localised server. Services such as Amazon Web Services or Microsoft Azure will have a much greater SLA and you will be a bit more self-sufficient compared to the standard dedicated or shared hosting solutions available.

Cloud based solutions also tend to be more secure than traditional hosting solutions, and for complete peace of mind ask your website developer to use a Content Distribution Network (CDN). A CDN is a large distributed network of servers deployed across a series of worldwide data centres. CDNs serve the static internet content (images, javascript and stylesheets) as well as downloadable documents (media files, software and documents) through their own cache and offload traffic served by your chosen web hosting server. CDNs can also protect against Denial of Service (DoS) attacks by absorbing the attack traffic across multiple locations. A DoS attack is when your website is purposefully overloaded with page requests in order to bog down and eventually crash a web server.

There are free CDN services available such as CloudFlare, BootstrapCDN and Incapsula. Microsoft Azure includes a CDN platform, as does Amazon through their CloudFront product.

IN SUMMARY

1 Check whether your chosen web agency has a site-launch checklist
2 Use Google Analytics (or your preferred analytics software) – it is imperative to audit your website's performance
3 Ask your web designer agency for a copy of their Service Level Agreement
4 Use a CDN for extra security and to lessen the load on server resources
5 Run a website audit yourself using the tools recommended in Part Four

STEP 9

What Happens If My Web Designer Gets Hit By A Bus?

We launched in 2004 and, as mentioned earlier in the book, we changed our business model during the 2007/2008 recession, to strengthen the business and secure a regular monthly cash flow. That made us feel pretty secure. However, as the recession took hold, the most common thing I was asked during my discovery sessions with customers was, 'What happens if you get hit by a bus', which reflected how wary people had become about where to spend their money.

That question continues to be asked frequently, so to answer it, I point out that we have survived the recession and gone on to strengthen our position by introducing the new business model.

I also point out that it is a level playing field and, as any web design agency or freelancer you approach has the same propensity to failure as the next organisation, anyone can get hit by that bus at any point. Do not forget, this is still an unregulated industry, which makes it a very risky business, with which to go into partnership. There are, however, lots of ways for a web design agency to mitigate those risks for their customers and ensure that they will be around for many years to come.

One of the biggest problems that our industry faces is that lack of regulation. What this means is that anyone can set themselves up with a copy of Dreamweaver on their laptop and call themselves a web designer; someone with no expertise in graphic design, domain name management, online strategy, hosting, backups or SEO. Would you trust someone to represent you in court if they had just, 'Read a few books on law' and called themselves a lawyer? I doubt it, so why treat one of the most important weapons in your marketing armoury in the same regard?

When hiring a new agency or freelancer check what contingency planning they have in place. Do they take regular server backups? What service level agreement do they have with their server provider? What happens if key staff get hit by a bus? If you choose to move provider will they help with the migration process?

The key to any website is the domain name registration. The domain redirects your website and email traffic to the relevant server, it's like the address for your house; without that you cannot get your post delivered. So, if you do employ the services of an agency or freelancer I would ensure that they have shared all of your domain registration details with you and that you have tested access to your domain's control panel using those credentials.

(↑) TOP TIP

Find a reliable domain registrar to manage your domains, they should have a really simple to use control panel, great customer support, plus no hidden fees to transfer domains or for support.

Registering the domain yourself has two benefits:

1   You will be paying direct for the domain – this is normally slightly cheaper than paying an agency to manage the domain on your behalf
2   You have access to the domain which means your website can easily be transferred to another provider in the event of a catastrophe

The downsides experienced by some of our customers, however, are:

1   Quite often they forget to enable the auto-renew, so their domain expires and the website/email stop working
2   Their credit card info expires, meaning that the domain is not always auto-renewed on time, resulting in down-time for the website/email
3   They forget their login information. It's recoverable, but it's a nuisance

If you run with an agency, then let them manage your domain as all of the billing and management is handled in one place.

 TOP TIP

If an agency or Freelancer registers your domain for you, double check that they have registered the domain in your name or business name. Your business should be the registered owner of the domain, however it is fine for your agency to be the registered Technical, Billing or Admin contact for the domain. Likewise if you decide to move they should never hold your domain ransom.

There are many other indicators of the actual resilience of your web designer. For example, how much are they charging for monthly hosting and support? A good agency will have a monthly fee for hosting and support. The greater the number of customers being supported and paying a monthly amount, the more stable the web design agency, and thus the more reliable for the customer. If a web designer has a good monthly cash flow it will ensure that they can cover the costs of their hosting solution easily, and update their servers whenever they need to ensure the best possible service. If this monthly income is not in place and they rely solely on project income, then what will happen to them if their sales pipeline dries up?

We charge a monthly support and hosting fee, and it covers all of our basic overheads, so even when things get a bit tight we know we will not be going out of business because we cannot afford to service your websites.

Find out where your website will be hosted. Ideally it should be held in a cloud based solution such as Amazon Web Services or Microsoft Azure, or in a well-established data-centre. Your website should *never* be hosted in a black box in your office or your web designer's office. Imagine; if there was something simple like a power cut or the telephone lines fail, your website would go down too.

Ask your website designer how they handle backups. They should mention something called RAID on their web server – RAID is a secondary hard drive on the server which holds a mirrored backup of the primary hard drive in the event it fails. We also take nightly backups of our customers' databases and weekly backups of their site files which are held both on-site and off-site.

Find out what technologies your web designer will be employing; what programming language they will be using to build your website. Ideally this should be one of the more widely supported programming languages such as PHP or ASP .Net. You may also recognise some of the more well-known Content Management Systems (CMS) such as WordPress, Joomla, Drupal, SiteCore, Sitefinity, Ubraco or Kentico; but don't be put off if your web designer has their own Web CMS, as long as it is written in a common language.

Finally, check who owns the Intellectual Property for your website, and for which bits. Sometimes agencies can be protective over releasing their CMS during a site transfer if you choose to move away from them, so ask the question, 'What IP do I own should I choose to move?' The simple answer to this should be, 'You own the site design, your content and images, and we have developed your website on an Open Source CMS platform so that is yours too.'

Over the last ten years we have lost only a handful of customers, and they have all had genuine reasons for wanting to migrate to another provider, such as relocation and the desire to use a local developer, which is absolutely fine. We *never* charge our customers for leaving us, and we make the process of transferring as simple and smooth as possible.

It is our way of thanking our customers for their continued support while they were with us.

IN SUMMARY

1 Find an established agency or freelancer

2 If you register your own domain or manage your own hosting solution find a reputable hosting provider (not the cheapest)

3 If your chosen agency registers a domain name on your behalf ensure it is registered in your name

4 Double check who owns the intellectual property for all aspects of your website

5 You should never be charged for changing providers if you have a genuine reason to leave

STEP 10

Launching Your Website

This is the most exciting part of the project. This is what all of the hours, days and weeks of planning, specification, proposal writing, design, development, content writing, testing and de-bugging have all been building up to. Finally your website is about to go live! Trying to get all of those last minute niggles ironed out can be quite a stressful time for you and your web designer.

This will be the point where a novice website designer might get tripped up, and this includes you if you've designed and built your website yourself. The processes of launching your website from the development to live environment can sometimes throw up some curve balls rendering a site which did work in development mode throwing up errors in the live environment.

 TOP TIP

Do not rush the launch of your website or leave it until the last minute.

There are a number of scenarios which make the launching of a website somewhat stressful. Here are some examples of what to avoid.

1   Change in scope – The process of designing and developing a website can sometimes be quite a long process. The chances of setting out a launch date at the start of that process and

expecting to hit it are quite slim; from experience most projects, on which we have worked, have involved some form of project scope creep which extends the design or development time and normally leads to overshooting the launch date. If you change the scope of your website during its development, expect the launch date to move accordingly.

2 Tight deadline – The website might be almost there but the customer wants to make a last minute change before their new website goes live. This is quite frustrating at 4.30pm on a Friday afternoon. Sometimes it is better just to wait until 9.30am on Monday to launch the website.

3 Sudden changes in deadline – Your web designer will hopefully quote a realistic timescale, within which to develop a website, but sometimes part way through the project the launch date will be brought forward because of something else happening within your business. This could be a marketing exercise, with which the website launch needs to coincide; their existing website or hosting provider might be ending their contract sooner than expected; you might be anticipating a meeting with a potential new customer and want to showcase your new website; or it could simply be impatience.

4 Domain name login – You get to the day of launch and for some reason the customer has either lost the login credentials for their domain name control panel or has changed the password to something else. Without the domain login information it is not possible to point the domain at the new website.

5 Last-minute testing – Sometimes last-minute testing does uncover a bug which hadn't been anticipated by anybody. If it is mission critical then it is better to abort the launch until the problem has been resolved. If it is not mission critical, switch the feature off, launch the website and publish the working feature post-launch.

6   Server bugs – If the development of the website has taken place on one server but is being deployed on another, you cannot always guarantee that the two servers will have the same configuration. You could deploy the website onto the live server and then find that there are bugs. Whenever possible, the development environment should be as close to that, on which the completed website will be deployed.

The worst part about this is that the customer tends to blame the developer for these sorts of problems. The developer can mitigate the risk of many of these problems by having a structured development path as well as setting realistic timescales and undertaking plenty of testing and de-bugging. They are, however, human beings and websites are a complex beast in many respects, because there are so many variables. My best advice is not to get disheartened if your site launch appears to be delayed. If the build has reached the stage where you are contemplating the launch of your website, most bugs can be ironed out quickly and easily and should only delay things by a matter of hours, or days at the very most.

Likewise there should be a 'roll back' option should your website launch with problems, so that you can quickly and easily pivot and revert back to a previous version if needs be. Ensure your developer has such a 'Plan B' just in case anything does go wrong when your website launches.

 TOP TIP

A website is an organic product, don't ever consider it to be finished.

Your website can always be improved through adding extra features and functionality. It can be enhanced through subtle design tweaks and you can change your customer journeys by moving a few buttons around and changing their colours. This means that when your new website launches it doesn't have to be perfect. Remember 'The Lean Startup'. Getting your website live sooner may save you some time because it gives you the opportunity to pivot if you've introduced an unpopular feature. I often get frustrated with my customers when they spend days making countless revision requests away from the original design because they feel that it will make a significant impact.

CASE STUDY: A local marketing agency had a project, which ran on for months at great expense because their customer was tweaking it to the nth degree. We convinced them that there was absolutely nothing wrong with putting a website live without all the features present. It enabled them to start eliciting feedback about the new website sooner. This meant they could pivot at a much earlier stage when the feedback received found the website wasn't quite right. They actually pivoted several times. Had they waited several months for the site to be perfect would have meant they couldn't elicit any feedback or start the feedback loop when they did. This saved valuable time, and most importantly, money.

⏻ TOP TIP

Google's PageRank is based on trust, the longer your website has been live the more it trusts you. If this is a new website, then get a holding page online immediately with your core message so that Google has something to index at the earliest possible stage. This gives you weeks or months head start when it comes to search engine optimisation.

Although rare, we've also had situations whereby it is not until the website has launched that it becomes apparent that a vital feature never made it into the customer's specification.

Design is very subjective and quite often changes are made by a company or organisation only to scratch their own itch, while forgetting about their customers. A 1pt change in font-size is not going to make a difference to whether someone purchases your products, but if your checkout feature is broken, which means they can't buy your products, that will make a huge difference. Many web design customers have to be reminded that they are not stuck with the website when the button is pushed for it to go live. It can be updated and new features added after it goes live; it is a constantly evolving commodity.

If there is any possibility of any downtime or disruption to your website or web application then it is better to plan to launch it at a non-critical time. If there is likely to be any disruption or if your new website is vastly different to your old website it is a good idea to warn your customers in advance that you are updating your website. This can be done with an article on your blog, twitter or Facebook status updates or via an email newsletter in advance of the new website launching.

You will likely require a training session on using your new CMS, so arrange this with your developer. They may include a one or two hour training session within their package, which may be delivered alongside video tutorials or a training manual. If additional training sessions are required, usually for larger organisations, then this time will likely be chargeable.

Timing for a site launch is critical. Try to avoid putting your websites live last thing on a Friday just in case there are any problems, because your developer might have gone home. Some web design agencies are open late or at weekends, but don't always expect that they will work to your business' opening hours. If it is essential to launch your site outside of your developer's normal working hours then expect that they may require payment for this time; especially if it is at three o'clock in the morning, when your site traffic is at its quietest!

The last hour before you or your developer leaves for a two week holiday is not, perhaps, the best time to go live with your website! If there happens to be a bug you could potentially be stuck with it for the whole two weeks. My advice is plan ahead and launch early if you can't wait until someone gets back from their holiday.

Once we have launched a website we run through a thorough site-launch check-list. In summary this involves:

- Testing your website thoroughly to ensure all of the pages and features are working
- Ensuring there are no broken links or missing images
- Thoroughly testing any specific features are working correctly (e.g. the blog, checkout, products, slideshows, etc)
- Testing email forms are submitting correctly and go to a Thank You page (for conversion tracking)
- Checking that Google Analytics is installed
- Testing the website on a multitude of web browsers and devices
- Ensure the website is configured correctly for the search engines
- Check that social media icons are linked up correctly
- Fixing any remaining standards validation errors
- Testing page load speeds using at least two different tools

There is a much more detailed site-launch checklist in Part Three of this book as well as an introduction, in Part Four, to all of the testing tools that we use.

Once your website has been launched and we are happy that it is working as intended and the site launch check list is complete we hold a debrief session with our client to sign the work off. This is a good opportunity to look at how well the project panned out and to ensure that our customer is happy. This is a good opportunity to start planning an Online Marketing Strategy with your web design agency.

We will agree on an appropriate time to review the website's progress in two or three months' time and start discussing 'Phase 2'. During the project you can guarantee that you will have developed a list of extra features that you want to see on the next version of the website, so we move these into Phase 2 and start the process all over again.

IN SUMMARY

1   Do not rush the launch of your website
2   A website is organic, it is never finished
3   Test your new website thoroughly and don't get too hung up on very minor details
4   Google's PageRank is based on trust built up over time therefore it might be a while before you start ranking in Google post launch
5   Implement the Site Launch Checklist laid out in Part 3 of the book, which follows next

PART THREE
SITE LAUNCH CHECKLIST

The *ultimate* to-do list when launching a new website

How to use this to-do list

This is a list of tests, checks, documents to look out for, pages to test as well as a reminder to set up tools such as Analytics and Webmaster tools. It is a comprehensive list.

Parts Four and Five in the book demonstrate how to test your website and set up social media correctly so you should be able to confidently identify any problems or errors on your new website.

However, if you have built your own website then I would recommend working through the more technically challenging tests with the help of a web designer.

HTML Validation: http://validator.w3.org/

CSS Validation: http://jigsaw.w3.org/css-validator/

Check for Javascript Errors:

Cross Browser Compatibility:

* IE 8+

* Firefox

* Safari

* Chrome

* Opera

* Mobile Browsers (iOS, Android etc)

Cross-platform Compatibility:

* Windows XP, Vista or 7 & 8

* Apple Mac OS X (Leapord 10.15 or above)

Evidence of Customised 404 Error Page:

Evidence of Sitemaps and Feeds:

- HTML sitemap
- sitemap.xml
- robots.txt
- urllist.txt/blog/feed.rss

Legal documents and footer links Present:

- Disclaimer
- Terms & Conditions of Website Usage
- Privacy Policy
- Copyright notice and correct year
- Cookie scripts

Test Dynamic Pages:

- Contact Form
- Blog Pages

Check Contact Information:

- Telephone Number
- Fax Number
- Email Address
- Address
- Registered Company Number
- Contact form functionality and target email

If Flash is Present:

- Check for noflash content

Submit site as Google Webmaster: http://www.google.com/webmasters

- Add verification code to meta tags

- Submit XML sitemap using webmaster tool

Set up Google Analytics: http://www.google.co.uk/analytics

Multiple domain and www to non-www redirect:

Test CMS using different user groups i.e. Uber, Editor, Admin etc:

Test website using SortSite:

Check website using WooRank: http://www.woorank.com/

Check website using Nibbler: http://nibbler.silktide.com/

Checked Social Media links:

- **Facebook**: http://www.facebook.com

- **Twitter**: http://twitter.com

- **LinkedIn**: http://www.linkedin.com

- **Google+:** https://plus.google.com/

Check Page Load Times using Google PageSpeed:

If you want to download my Site Launch Checklist please visit: http://www.onlinebusinessstartup.co.uk/downloads

PART FOUR
REVIEW

Take control of optimising the performance of *your* website

STEP 1

Why Review Your Own Website?

I run monthly workshops showing my customers how to audit their own websites, and they have presented several reasons to me as to why they attend.

1 Empowerment

If you are paying your web developer to design and build you a website you would hope that it would be done to a high standard. Given that our industry is unregulated, how can you guarantee that what has been built is good quality? It is useful to have a small armoury of free tools in your back pocket that you can turn to in order to review the quality of your own website. You can spend half an hour testing your website using the free tools which I will introduce you to shortly and be sure about the quality of your website.

When you view your new website, it may look great at first glance, but how do you know if it is performing well behind the scenes? At the very least, if the web designer has done a good job, you will gain great peace of mind by testing it – especially if it scores highly!

Re-empower yourself and do not become complacent by assuming that, because you have paid a professional to do a job, that they will do it well. Building a website which contains errors and is hosted on an ancient server can have a major impact and is like a building a house on weak foundations. At the outset you have a wonderfully beautiful new home, but the cracks will soon start showing and eventually it will simply fall over.

I have viewed and tested thousands of websites and I cannot recall one without a single area that could somehow benefit from improvement. Even my own website. You should feel empowered in the process of testing your own website. Although it may be small, it is a good feeling to gain an insight of some sort into what goes into the building of a website.

2 Speed

Your web design agency may be juggling several projects at any one time, and so it is possible that they may not always be able to give you the immediate response that you require. Outside of office hours, you might be preparing for a promotion of some kind, but may not have access to your developer to help you. Most websites these days are built upon a CMS framework which allows you to add content and build pages yourself. Being able to upload a new page of content and then immediately test it using one of the many tools available provides an immediate solution.

It just provides peace of mind that you have done the job properly, and hopefully your web developer will be pleased to see that you have done such a good job.

 TOP TIP

Remember that your agency has many customers and sometimes might not be able to react as quickly as you might like. Be accountable for the quality of your website(s) – you are, after all, the owner.

3 Cost Saving

If you are running your website on a bit of a tight budget then uploading and testing your web pages will save you some money because you won't have to pay your developer to do the updates for you. Rather than having to pay your developer to subscribe to the tools and then for the time taken to run the tests, it is something you can do yourself and then just present a list of updates you would like carried out.

It is much easier, and therefore cheaper, for a developer to do a larger batch than a multitude of individual updates.

4 Confidence

Having the confidence that your website is doing exactly what it is supposed to is very reassuring. Our customers rely on us to do a good job for them so that they don't have to worry about their website beyond their promotional and marketing exercises. Being able to evaluate your own website's performance against pre-defined benchmarks means that when your site reaches those benchmarks you can forget about it (for a short time at least).

Depending on the relationship you have with your developer, this can be a diplomatic way of raising issues that you have found with your website. I have come across some very arrogant developers in the past who are assured that their way is the best. Showing your developer the results of a test can be quite a subtle way of showing them that they have created a seven out of ten for you and not a ten out of ten.

I have seen it all:

- Link building campaigns which result in no inbound links
- Social media campaigns, where the website isn't linked up to the social media profiles properly
- Pay-per-click advertising on a website with no analytic accounts installed
- Copy-written web pages with typos, spelling mistakes and grammatical errors
- Search engine optimised pages of content with no H1 tag

Use the free testing tool available and get some confidence back that your website has been built correctly.

5 Insight

The tools which I am going to introduce you to will give you a bit of an insight into the building blocks that go into a website behind the scenes. Typically a website visitor will judge their interaction with your website on two criteria:

1. How good the website looks
2. Whether they found what they were looking for

They will likely have no idea why or how they ended up on your website beyond typing a search phrase into Google and finding your website (hopefully) on the first page of the results. Using the testing tools will begin to unravel how you get a website onto the first page of Google in the first place.

I will caveat this now; I am not an SEO specialist and will never profess to be one. I believe in building websites properly using the standards compliance that has been determined by W3C. I have had a great amount of success by building great websites for my customers, ensuring that all of the boxes have been ticked. This has been enough to sustain my business and my clients' businesses.

Using tools like Nibbler, Sortsite, GTMetrix and Pingdom will give you a small insight into what goes into building a website. The quality of the code, which is output, and the number of inbound links; the relationship between social media and your website; the structure of your content from headings, page descriptions and images, to how you name your page URLs, printability and how offensive your content is.

If nothing else I want to raise awareness that it is not all about design, and adding a checkout to your website, but as your website scales, it will also be about the minutest of details such as the colour of the call-to-action buttons and how quickly visitors were able to complete the checkout process.

6 Inquisitive

The monthly workshops I run with my customers are filled with people because they are inquisitive. They want to know a little bit more about what we do and how we go about building their website. They have no compulsion to build the website themselves, but are interested in understanding a bit more about their website and most importantly how they can better interact with it.

Personally I have no hesitation about giving my customers free access to check up on me. Returning to point 2, about speed, if I am up against it time wise, it saves me a job if my customers are also auditing their own websites and pointing out anything that we may have missed. We are human after all. One of the biggest problems we face is the constantly evolving web technologies available and there is so much choice. Our customers sometimes discover emerging technologies that we may have missed, which is very helpful.

Developers and designers generally have good and bad habits, but our customers tend to be very consistent from an analytical perspective especially when it comes to analysing their own websites. This is the best way to wheedle out the poor developers because through your own inquisitiveness you will likely now find plenty of problems with your own website which your developer had no idea existed. Perhaps if you build the website yourself this might be the prompt required to consider speaking to a professional web design agency or expert.

STEP 2

What Are We Testing For?

While you are going through the testing and auditing process it is worthwhile understanding what it is that you are testing for. This is where things take a turn towards the technical sphere but I will do my best to unravel a few website mysteries for you without talking coding and three-letter acronyms; for now anyway.

We are now in the day and age where everyone has a website in the 'connected' and 'always on' world. It is not just about having a good or mediocre website, it is actually about having a great website. This is especially true because we are moving into the era of the mobile dominated market place. We need to ensure that if our customers are looking at our websites on smartphones and mobile devices that there is no degradation of service. In the web technology sphere we are now talking about 'mobile first' technology where, for the first time, web designers are considering designing for mobile devices first before standard monitor sizes because soon they will be more commonly used.

In the last chapter I talked about good looking websites which worked. This is the minimum our customers expect now of a website. So in order to get an edge on our competition we need to consider several keys areas of our website's development:

1 Page Loading Speeds

Consider the seven second rule whereby you have approximately five to seven seconds to grab someone's attention, tell them who you are and what you do from the moment that they first land on your website. If you fail to achieve that milestone then you will lose that customer before they've even had time to forget who you are. They will likely return to the search provider, go to a competitor or check Facebook. Worse still if your page takes longer than 7 seconds to load in the first place (i.e. 7 seconds before anything appears on-screen) then they won't even have the opportunity to forget who you are because they never got to see your website in the first place.

Web pages have three core layers:

1 Basic Code Layer – this is your basic layer of content (HTML code) and is displayed first
2 Graphics – your images and page styles are then loaded, this determines the layout, font styles, images and colours
3 Whizzy Stuff – this is where elements begin to move on screen by way of slideshows, videos and social media feeds

Ideally you want your basic layer and graphics to load up as soon as possible. Your customers are generally willing to wait a little bit longer to see the whizzy bits appearing on your website. They know these files are bigger in size.

2 Web Standards Compliance

The World Wide Web Consortium (W3C) are the organisation who have determined how the web is going to be built. The purpose of web standards is to ensure that web pages are displayed in a consistent fashion based on a core set of principles and components.

This is our rule book which determines the quality of our code and whether it contains any errors.

Imagine the code which is generated by your CMS is spat out by your web server. That code is read by two very important readers:

1. Search Engines like Google, Bing, Yahoo!, Ask & AOL
2. Web Browsers such as Chrome, Internet Explorer, Safari, Opera & Firefox

The search engines determine how search engine friendly your website is, and the web browsers will determine how easy your web page is to display. This code is like a book in some respects. If you have typos, missing sentences or words and grammatical errors then naturally a book is much harder to read. The same goes for HTML. If it is not standards compliant and is littered with errors then search engines and web browsers will find it hard to read your code. They have to start filling the gaps, and quite often get it wrong. We have an opportunity here to feed information to search engines and web browsers to ensure that they are being interpreted as we had intended.

3 Quality of Content

Here we want our content to be readable by the widest possible audience, and the search engines look at the quality of your content and build this score into their algorithm to determine the overall quality of each page of content.

1 **Reading Age** – Search engines look at your content and determine its reading age based on a number of factors including the length of words, sentences and paragraphs as well as how technical your content is. The longer everything gets then the higher the reading age will be. However, you want your reading age to be as low as possible. The lowest reading age is the equivalent of an eleven year-old. The higher your reading age goes the more of your target audience you are potentially cutting out.

Think of this as an extension of the seven second rule here; you've got someone's attention and they have started to read your content, but the readability is too difficult, which means they will leave. If the user can quickly scan through your content and understand it then you have more chance of the message sticking.

2 Meta Information – This is your 'Page Title' and 'Page Description'. The best way to demonstrate this is by example. If you do a Google search, the text in blue, which links to your page content, is the 'Title' and the 'Description' appears in black underneath. Both of these need to be natural language text and including your page keywords.

HostPipe Website Design Stroud, Gloucestershire Web ...
www.hostpipe.co.uk/ ▾
HostPipe Website Design and Development Services in Stroud, Gloucestershire Web Services. Call 01453 884100 for more information.
You've visited this page many times. Last visit: 22/06/14

 TOP TIP

You can preview all of the pages which Google has indexed, by searching for your domain preceded by the keyword 'site:' e.g. 'site:coconutstrategy.com'. This will give you a list of all of the pages that Google has indexed on your website, including your Page Titles and Descriptions.

3 Headings – There are several layers of heading ranging from H1 to H6. Every web page should have one Heading 1 or <h1> tag. You can then nest multiple Heading 2 (or <h2>) and Heading 3 (<h3>) underneath your initial headings with Paragraphs (<p>) between headings. Your <h1> should include your page keywords and reflect the content of the page to come.

4 Spelling Mistakes – Google is very intelligent and spell-checks your website. If your website has a higher than average error ratio then you will be penalised. This is because it is likely to be comparing your page of content to another page of content with no spelling errors.

4 On-Site Search Engine Optimisation (SEO)

In short we code websites from the ground up to ensure that they are search engine friendly. This means that we are making it as quick and simple as possible for the Googlebot to index our site pages and then parse through each web page. The parsing of the web page is dealt with by adhering to standards compliance and ensuring that your page content is well structured.

The indexing side of things is more complicated. The first thing Google looks for is a file called the robots.txt. Within the robots file we will place details about which directories and pages we are happy for Google to index and to exclude from its index. The robots file also allows you to block entire search engines from indexing your website if you so wish. We also place a link to the sitemap.xml file within the robots file. The sitemap.xml contains a list of all of the pages on your website including:

- Page URL (or file path)
- Last time that file was modified
- A priority (ranging from 1.0 – most important to 0 – least important)
- Change frequency – how often we expect to update the page

These two files are designed to make it as easy as possible for Google and friends to index your website. Otherwise it has to crawl its way through your website picking out links which is hard work. If we make

Google's life slightly easier, it might help us.

Finally you want to ensure that you have a custom 404 Error Page. A 404 page appears when a page has been deleted or moved. Sometimes you get a really basic 404 with not much extra information. Or ideally you could create a 404 error page which is a bit more fun from a design perspective and keeps your audience engaged.

Ideally though, your 404 error page should have a sitemap; so your site visitors have the option of navigating to another page on their website if the page they are trying to find doesn't exist.

Not only do your customers get to see a 404 error, but the server returns a 404 status code which is what Google sees. Google rates you on what errors you are providing to your customers so it checks to see whether you are serving the correct 404 error status for pages which no longer exist.

You can do a simple test to see whether these three files exist on your website by adding a file path to the end of your domain URL:

- http://www.YOURDOMAIN.com/robots.txt
  (e.g. http://coconutstrategy.com/robots.txt)
- http://www.YOURDOMAIN.com/sitemap.xml
  (e.g. http://coconutstrategy.com/sitemap.xml)
- http://www.YOURDOMAIN.com/aethasrthat
  (e.g. http://coconutstrategy.com/aethasrthat)

5 Off-Site SEO

Offsite SEO looks at metrics such as:

- Link-building – how many inbound links your website has and from how many individual websites. Search engines also consider how relevant the sites are that are linking to your website and the 'anchor text' used to link to your website.
- Social media marketing – how much is your website being liked and shared? And the connections between your social media profiles (such as LinkedIn, Facebook, Google+ and Twitter) and your website.
- Popularity – How many people are navigating to and viewing your website and how often.

It is important to stress how much the off-site SEO sphere has changed over time. When the Internet was first born it was all about the Meta Keywords field, which most people soon spammed and it started to give false results. Then as the Internet grew through its early childhood, and more websites were created, links started to appear between websites and web pages. So, that is what Google then used as its primary metric in its algorithm. Now the Internet is grown up we are in a social age, and Google ranks Social Media sharing much more highly than link building, to the extent that keywords are now virtually ignored by most search engines, and inbound links only contribute a tiny portion of PageRank.

⏻ BIGGEST TIP EVER!

It amazes me that I have customers who walk into my office and tell me that they don't want to entertain a social media campaign because, 'Who's going to buy my products on Facebook?' I provide them with the explanation above. We do not create social media profiles because we are going to post a picture of your product on Facebook and thousands of people are going to buy it because of that. We do it mainly to keep the search engines happy. More importantly, we do it with Google+ to keep Google happy.

Google takes 90% of the search engine traffic. Most people don't realise that YouTube is the 2nd biggest search engine after Google...and it's owned by Google. Google owns Google+ and also gives you Google Analytics for FREE.

Use Social Media tools, which are also free, and more importantly use all Google's tools which it provides for free.

6 Cross Browser Compatibility

The five most popular web browsers are Chrome, Internet Explorer, Opera, Safari and Firefox. These are the applications which you use to browse the internet with. They take the code which a web developer has created and turn it into the visual website which you see in front of you.

What we want to achieve is for your website to display correctly in as many different web browsers as possible. If for any reason your website doesn't display correctly or doesn't display at all then you might be alienating the potential customers who are using those browsers.

There are a number of websites counting down the final lifespan of various version of Internet Explorer as this has traditionally been the hardest web browser to please over the years. IE7 was recently deprecated and now the Internet Explorer 8 Countdown has begun: http://theie8countdown.com/.

Google and the various search engines also know if your website isn't cross browser compatible.

7 Cross Device Compatibility (Responsiveness)

Not only does our website have to work on a variety of web browsers but it also needs to work on a multitude of different devices. This now includes smartphones, tablets, laptops and PCs. The term responsiveness is derived from the website (interfaces) needing to respond (display) on a variety of screen sizes and resolutions. The mobile market already accounts for 40% of the people browsing the internet. Creating a website which doesn't work on anything but a desktop now means you are immediately restricting your potential audience by 40%. If you owned a shop, would you stand at the door and refuse 40% of your customers entry? Definitely not, so why do it with your website?

Search engines also test whether you have created a responsive version of your website...you get the picture now?

8 Accessibility

Accessibility is probably the most overlooked element of optimising a website. In fact it should not be classified within optimising a website because it is discriminatory not to make best efforts to ensure that your website is accessible. Accessibility is quite a broad subject; Accessibility is the degree to which a product, device, service, or environment is available to as many people as possible. Accessibility in the online world focuses on people with disabilities or special needs. This accounts for a large portion of your potential target market, up to 20% and includes website visitors with visual impairments, motor problems, learning difficulties and hearing impairments.

Close your eyes and imagine for one moment that you are navigating through your website. You need to 'read' the text on a particular page and complete a specific task such as buy a product or submit an enquiry form.

There are many assistive technologies available to help individuals with disabilities browse the web such as screen readers, Braille printers, screen magnification and keyboard overlays. However there are specific ways of coding a website in order to communicate between the website and the assistive technologies.

Conclusion

From experience following best practices and creating a standards compliant website gets you most of the way towards ensuring that you have met at least the minimum level of accessibility, cross browser and device compatibility and search engine friendliness.

It is natural for a website to degrade over time because the knowledge gap between the designer/developer and their customers is vast. Using the tools in the next step I want to start bridging that gap and educating business owners and experienced developers alike that we need to be working towards Standards Compliance.

STEP 3

The Seven Best Tools for Auditing Your Website for FREE

Nibbler

Nibbler is a free tool for testing websites, created by a well-regarded company in the field of website design, Silktide.

Entering the address of any website into Nibbler and it will give you a report scoring the website out of 10 for various important criteria including accessibility, SEO, social media and technology. *Overall we are aiming to achieve a score of 8.0 or above.*

Nibbler is a free tool which enables you to get loads of information about your website without having to pay for anything. It allows you to test up to 5 pages of your website for free; however, if you want even more information, you might want to consider upgrading to Sitebeam which is Silktide's more detailed (Premium) website testing software.

[source – http://nibbler.silktide.com]

PageScoring

You have approximately seven seconds to grab someone's attention and tell them 'who you are' and 'what you do'. If you fail to achieve that within seven seconds then it is likely that person may get bored and potentially leave your website to visit one of your competitors.

Likewise, if your website doesn't load at all within seven seconds then you've got even bigger problems. **When a website fails to load it is unlikely that a site visitor will ever return.**

What we are aiming to achieve is for the most important web page content to load within the first second or two, and then for the rest of the code which does all the whizzy stuff to load within the next three to four seconds.

PageScoring's online web tool – Website Speed Test – is designed to provide website owners with valuable information about the loading speed of their domain and website. This tool will check everything from your domain resolving speed to your download times.

The time it takes for your website to load to your visitors is very important. In fact, according to a survey, almost 50% of visitors expect a website to load in two seconds or less, and 40% of visitors abandon a website that takes more than three seconds to load.

[source – http://www.pagescoring.com/website-speed-test/]

GTMetrix

GTmetrix uses Google Page Speed and Yahoo! YSlow to grade your site's performance and provides actionable recommendations to fix these issues.

In terms of Search Engine Optimisation (SEO), Google is hinting at using Page Speed score in its ranking algorithm. As developers and marketers look to optimise their sites, page speed should be among the top optimisations to consider.

[source – http://gtmetrix.com]

Pingdom

Pingdom built this Website Speed Test to help you analyse the load speed of your websites and learn how to make them faster. It lets you identify what about a web page is fast, slow, too big, what best practices you're not following, and so on. Pingdom have tried to make it useful both to experts and novices alike.

In short, Pingdom wanted it to be an easy-to-use tool to help webmasters and web developers everywhere optimize the performance of their websites.

Examine all parts of a web page – View file sizes, load times, and other details about every single element of a web page (HTML, JavaScript and CSS files, images, etc.). You can sort and filter this list in different ways to identify performance bottlenecks.

Performance overview – Pingdom automatically put together plenty of performance-related statistics for you based on the test result

Performance grade and tips – See how your website conforms to performance best practices from Google Page Speed (similar to Yahoo's Yslow). You can get some great tips on how to speed up your website this way.

Trace your performance history – Pingdom save each test for you so you can review it later and also see how things change over time (with pretty charts!).

Test from multiple locations – See how fast a website loads in Europe, the United States, etc.

Share your results – Pingdom has made it easy for you to perform a test and share it with your friends, work colleagues or web host.

How it works

All tests are done with real web browsers, so the results match the end-user experience exactly. Pingdom uses a bunch of instances of Google's Chrome web browser to load websites, record performance data, and so on. Tests are done from dedicated Pingdom servers.

[source – http://tools.pingdom.com/fpt/]

SortSite

SortSite is a one-click web site testing tool used by a wide variety of businesses and independent agencies. The tool is available as a subscription web application and a desktop application.

One click is all it takes to analyse an entire web site. Each page is checked against 450+standards based checkpoints.

Benefits

Problems like broken links, spelling errors and usability problems drive visitors away from your site. Search engine issues stop visitors before they arrive. Find and fix website problems before your customers find them.

[source – http://try.powermapper.com/]

W3C Validation Tool

The World Wide Web Consortium (W3C) is an international community where Member organizations, a full-time staff, and the public work together to develop Web standards. Led by Web inventor

Tim Berners-Lee and CEO Jeffrey Jaffe, W3C's mission is to lead the Web to its full potential.

The W3C validation tool evaluates your website's conformance with W3C open standards to quickly identify those portions of your website that need your attention

The W3C have just launched a Premium service to check all of the pages of your website: https://validator-suite.w3.org/

[source – http://validator.w3.org/]

Wave Accessibility Tool

You can be fined if your website is found to be discriminatory against people with disabilities in the same way as any of the physical elements of your office or business.

Not only that but 20% of web users have some form of disability, so imagine that your website is not accessible; you are automatically reducing your potential target audience down by a further 20%. If you get 10,000 unique visitors per month that could be as many as 2,000 individual customers who may choose to go elsewhere.

[source – http://wave.webaim.org/]

- See more at: http://coconutstrategy.com/blog/2014/06/the-7-best-tools-for-testing-your-website/

STEP 4

Google Analytics

Analytics tools are important because you've gone through all the hard work of getting your business strategy organised and implemented, finding the best web developer you can and making your online presence is as good as it can be. One of the SMART objectives involves ensuring that your objectives are measurable. Seeing how your site's traffic is performing means that you can start a feedback loop, make changes to your website and then see whether it has had a positive or negative impact on your website traffic. You can also start to measure the impact other marketing activities have on your website traffic.

Google Analytics allows you to view your website's performance down to the minute detail. Not to mention it is another useful free tool provided by Google so where possible I encourage our customers to use Google Analytics. There are lots of other analytics tools available, but Google Analytics is my tool of choice.

 TOP TIP

One of the reasons why I encourage the use of Google Analytics is because of the influence it has on the indexing of web pages in Google's search product. When you add a new page of content, and then view it in the browser with Analytics installed on your website. Google automatically adds the page into its list of pages to index. This alleviates the need to either do a manual submission or wait for Google to look at your updated sitemap.xml file.

Setting Up

The process of setting up Google Analytics is relatively straightforward, but you may require the help of a web developer or someone who is au fait with HTML and Javascript:

1 Register for a Google account – tip: you can use any email address not just a GMail address at this point
2 Register for a Google Analytics account – follow the setup wizard
3 Google then presents you with a snippet of javascript code which you need to include on every page of your website
4 Check that you have installed the analytics code correctly, check your analytics after twenty-four hours; you should start to see some activity in your feed.

Unique Visitors

The most important metric to look at on analytics is the number of unique visitors visiting your website on a daily, weekly or monthly basis. There are some great filtering tools which allow you to average data out and get a simple overview of traffic so that you can start to set benchmarks. Google recently changed this to users and 'sessions'. Users are unique site visitors but they may have logged a number of sessions on your website over a period of time. A common mistake is to talk about hits, but on a page by page basis a hit could include image files, javascript files and a number of other elements on a page. So one page visit could equal 50 hits. Which is misleading.

TOP TIP

Your computer's IP address will register as a session on your analytics which affects the stats. You can set up filters on Analytics to filter out specific network IP addresses.

Page Views, Duration and Bounce Rate

Page views and average duration per session are very important. You have seven seconds to grab someone's attention and tell them who you are, what you do and to hopefully engage with them. If the user leaves without engaging with your website then this is called a 'bounce'. A bounce is considered to be a site visitor not engaging with your website for a period of thirty minutes from the start of the session. Google displays this in its bounce rate metric, i.e. if your site experiences 100 visitors, and there are twenty bounces, your bounce rate will be 20%. Ideally you want someone to visit several pages of your website and actively engage with the site for a minute or two or more if possible.

Demographics

Further down the page you can start to break the data down by language, country and web browser so you can start to build a profile of your website visitors. This is useful; if 80% of your visits are from mobile devices and your website is not responsive then this is a good indicator that your next website task is to make your website responsive.

If you are targeting your SEO campaign on localised searches (e.g. electricians in Gloucestershire) you can also see the cities from where searches are originating. So if you are hitting Stroud, Cheltenham, Gloucester and Cirencester then your campaign is working. If Gloucester, Massachusetts pops up in the list then perhaps there is a problem.

Real-time Overview

Being a complete data geek, the real-time overview allows you to see how many people are looking at your website right now. You can follow which pages they are looking at, how long they spend on them (roughly) and what search keywords they used to find your web page. Although if you have a low traffic website then this may not be for you as you might have to wait a while for that first visitor to pop up in the real-time screen.

Goal Conversions

Your web developer may need to help you get goal conversions set up. Goal conversions are triggered when specific pre-defined actions happen on your website. This could include when a site visitor:

- submits an enquiry form
- buys a product
- completes a newsletter signup form
- downloads a PDF document

Funnels

You can link a series of goals together to create a funnel and then measure touch points where visitors drop out of the funnel. So this might be:

- Customer looked at a product
- Added it to their basket
- Completed the address details
- Added credit card information
- Completed the checkout

This is incredibly useful; if 75% visitors (or whatever benchmark you choose) of visitors drop out at the address stage perhaps there is a problem with the address section of the checkout process which you need to address:

- is it buggy?
- is it complicated?
- are there too many form fields?
- does it appear on a smartphone?

If you improve one part of the funnel and this dropout rate is decreased this will enable the goal conversion rate to increase. The maths are simple; this means more successful goal conversions – i.e. SALES.

Keyword (Not Provided) Workaround
OK, so you've logged into Google Analytics, stumbled your way through to where you're expecting to see the list of keywords people have used to land on your website...

- **Hint:** Acquisitions -> Keywords -> Organic

And finally you will see a list of keywords which is topped by the keyword 'Not Provided'; typically this accounts for 80%+ of your keyword traffic.

Why does Google Analytics display keywords as '(not provided)'
Well the answer is relatively simple, many people now have an account registered with Google. It's helpful because it puts shortcuts on the Google landing page to your most frequently visited websites. However, the reason why it's not helpful is because when someone is

logged into their Google Account and they perform an organic search it sends the search request over a secure layer which is encrypted. This they assure us is for privacy reasons, but it prevents the search query from being passed on to your website where the Google Analytics code is triggered and keywords are stored, which is why they end up in the (not provided) bin in Google Analytics.

So, how do I find out what keywords people are finding my Website for?

Ironically the answer lies within another Google product, Google Webmaster Tools:

[source – http://www.google.com/webmasters/]

It's another free tool from Google and you will need to verify with Google that you are indeed the webmaster of the website by placing another snippet of code within your site files – they do provide neat instructions or ask your website developer to take care of this for you.

Once you have verified your domain you can then navigate to your website's dashboard -> Search Traffic -> Search Queries and voila, the search queries entered into Google will be displayed.

This really useful tool also demonstrates a great deal more useful information about the search terms users have been entering to land on your website including:

- Number of Impressions
- Clicks
- Click Through Rate (CTR) %
- Average Position of the Keyword

Review, Report and Analyse

⏻ TOP TIP

Once a month look at your analytics traffic and produce some reports which are geared around your business; analyse these reports during your monthly strategy meetings. Make sure that you find at least one thing to improve on your website from the analytics traffic.

Hopefully your website traffic will be consistent at least, if not going up. If there is a sudden decline in web traffic then you have an immediate action to undertake to find out why traffic has gone down. You can see if traffic is seasonal and whether your other marketing activities are having an impact on website traffic. If goal conversions drop off a cliff perhaps there is an error in the checkout process. If traffic shoots up does it correlate with a highly retweeted tweet you posted during the month?

⏻ TOP TIP

Make your web developer accountable if there is a significant change in your site traffic. However, also be mindful if you've made a number of content changes this will have an impact on your site's pagerank. It may not actually be your web developer's fault that traffic has changed but he/she will be able to explain to you why the traffic is the way it is.

PART FIVE
SOCIAL MEDIA

Content Strategy, Scheduling and Automation

INTRODUCTION TO SOCIAL MEDIA

Social media is now the top pagerank indicator that search engines use within their algorithms. When the internet first started to become popular the meta keywords field used on every page of content was considered to be the most important HTML entity to complete. What the search engines realised, and perhaps not quickly enough, was that people were gaming the meta keywords field.

Your competitors could also look at your meta keywords field and copy it in order to compete with you in the organic search engine rankings. Google* eventually deprecated that from their algorithm and now they have chosen not to use it as a search engine metric within their algorithm at all. I still recommend our clients add it in as a matter of good house-keeping though and some search engines still consider the meta keyword field.

From here Google started to become a bit more intelligent and look at inbound links as a metric in their algorithm. Link scoring is based on the number of websites linking to your own websites and the number of links within those websites which link to your website. Over time Google started to appraise relevance when ranking links ensuring that links came from websites and pages of content within websites with relevant content to your own.

Eventually, like meta keywords, people started to find ways of gaming links. By outsourcing link building to paid-for link farms, directories and forums, thus lessening the relevance and naturally lowering their own pagerank. More fool them. Links replaced keywords as the highest scoring algorithm marker. Now Google needed to look for new markers to introduce into their algorithm to replace the gamed link farms.

Naturally as Social Media started to proliferate, the see-saw rocked in the favour of social media becoming one of the major markers in Google's algorithm.

What I hope to achieve through the final part of this book is to:

1   Provide an introduction to the 'big four' social media platforms:-Facebook, Google+, LinkedIn and Twitter
2   Creating the perfect profile
3   How to test whether you have set these pages up correctly
4   Social Media Content Strategy
5   Scheduling and Automation

* I talk about Google quite a lot when referring to Search Engines in general. This is purely because in the UK and US markets Google takes a vast majority of the search engine traffic. There are other search engines available such as Yahoo, Bing, Ask etc

STEP 1

Facebook

The most widely used social media platform is Faceboook. At the time of writing:

- Facebook had over 1,3bn active users
- The average user spends 18 minutes per session when they check Facebook

I will be focusing on setting up a Facebook Page in order to help promote your business using a series of Top Tips.

How to Register and Set Up a Facebook Page for a Business

http://www.wikihow.com/Create-a-Facebook-Page-for-a-Business

Logo and Branding

When you create assets for your various social media profiles I ensure that I have a set of brand guidelines available to reference and that I have several different versions of my logo available to use. Depending on the shape and aspect ratio (size/orientation) of your logo, I recommend having a horizontal and vertical stack of your logo as well as a square version of your emblem or icon in PNG and JPG formats. Most social media platforms require a version of your logo or a square avatar so ensure they are easily accessible and upload-able.

Having a common set of brand guidelines to refer to ensures that the look and feel of each of your social media profiles is consistent. This means that no matter what form your potential customers see your business in it is instantly recognisable regardless of where they chose to engage or make their buying decision.

Banner Image

We have a hero shot (banner) image on our website home page, which we ensure is reflected on Facebook to ensure the core message and brand is consistent.

Editing the Page

To edit your page, if you click on your 'About' section you should then see a small edit link in the top right hand corner of the bio. When you click on that you will be presented with a left hand menu with a series of links on the right hand side. If those links appear as blue link it means you haven't filled out all of the info. So, make sure you complete all of the available fields.

Do not shirk on filling out this information. Fill out all of the fields in detail. It helps your end-customers and also search engines.

It allows you to fill out all of your contact details, including address, telephone number, email, website address and even opening hours. Fill it all out. You want to make it as easy as possible for potential customers to engage with you. Completing the address field triggers the mapping facility on Facebook to appear on your profile.

Common Mistake

One of the most common mistakes people make when completing their Facebook profile is to enter their website address into the About

Us text. Facebook provides a specific website URL field. Filling this out means that the search engines can easily reference whether your Facebook page links back to your website.

Shorten URL

When you first set up a Facebook page you are assigned a complicated Facebook URL. At the earliest possibility choose a customised Facebook URL which reflects your organisation's brand i.e. https://www.facebook.com/CoconutStrategy

Strategy

1 Create engaging content on your Facebook time line
2 Link to industry related news which your customers might engage with
3 Write engaging blog articles and link back to them from Facebook
4 Upload testimonials from customers and ask them to complete 'reviews' on your Facebook page
5 Upload images of products or services which you have supplied to your customers

Build up your page with a series of interesting posts which showcase your work and area of expertise.

The key thing to remember here is that your website is likely to be the strongest tool for converting potential customers into warm leads. If they happen to find you initially through your Facebook page then it should be a true reflection of your business but funnel the user through to your website.

Your Website

As well as liking your Facebook page, you can embed Facebook icons on your website and invite users to 'like' specific pages of content on your website. Remember Google is using Social Media markers in its algorithm which take many different forms:

1 Do you have a Facebook page?
2 Does it link correctly to your website?
3 Does your website link correctly to your Facebook page?
4 Do people share your Facebook posts?
5 Do your web pages generate page 'likes' independently?

Each of these contributes individually to your PageRank.

Benefits

- Facebook is FREE
- It helps with SEO (if you set it up correctly)
- Networking and Research
- Facebook Insights (once you've accumulated 30 page likes)

Downsides

1 Facebook owns the right to re-use all of the content which you upload (including images)
2 If Facebook went out of business or choose to close down then all of your data will disappear with them
3 Facebook is now focussing on monetising their offering, especially for businesses

Reach and Post Boost

When you post something you will see in the bottom left corner of the post a metric called 'reach'. This is the total number of people who have seen your status update. You may have 15,000 page likes but your reach may only be 150. This is because Facebook only puts your posts in front of the audience who they feel you will engage with. If you want to increase your reach you have to 'boost' your post with paid-for advertising.

This means that Facebook is free for individuals, but businesses must pay a premium to have their goods and services put in front of a very wide potential target audience.

STEP 2

Twitter

Twitter is the second most widely used social media platform, at the time of writing:

- there are over 650 million active users over 58 million tweets sent per day

It is the easiest out of the four major social media platforms to set up because there is very little information which needs to be added. This presents its own set of challenges though because you need to be really succinct with your biography.

How to Register and Set Up a Twitter Account

http://www.wikihow.com/Make-a-Twitter-Account

Common Question

The most common question I get asked about Twitter is, 'Do you set up a twitter account up for your personal or business brand? How do you differentiate the two?' I usually remind customers to return to their business strategy, and are they promoting themselves as an individual or their business brand. That acts as a steer for the style and type of Twitter profile you set up. Within larger organisations set up several twitter accounts for their business which reflect different department functions; i.e. Support, HR, PR, Announcements etc plus individuals within the organisation will have personal twitter profiles but reflecting their role within the business. SME's do not tend to have departments and may only be one person, so my question is, 'Why would you need two Twitter accounts?'

Brand and Identity

As per Facebook you need to ensure that your brand is consistent with your website and other social media profiles. There are two images which are important to upload:

1 **The banner image** – make this consistent with the hero shot you use on your website and on your other social media profiles
2 **Your avatar** – this can either be your company emblem or a professional head shot depending on how you answered the common question

Account Name and @handle

The account name will be your company's name or your own name depending on your answer to the common question, and is fully customisable to match your brand. The @handle is used to identify users by a unique name on Twitter. Sometimes your company name may already be taken as an @handle unless your name or company name is truly unique. But if @RobinMWaite is gone maybe choose @RobinMWaiteUK or @OfficialRobinWaite instead.

Biography

Your bio is quite short and limited to only 160 characters so you need to be snappy. Use your elevator pitch, if you have one and again keep the core message consistent with each of your social media profiles. #tags are used to mark keywords or topics in a Tweet. It was created organically by Twitter users as a way to categorise messages. I recommend ending your bio with a few #tags to demonstrate topics within your niche which you might be tweeting about.

Location

This is a simple text entry field, you can put anything in here but I recommend putting in the location(s) in which you commonly carry out your work.

Website Address

 TOP TIP

Make sure you fill this out. Search engines use this field as a marker when checking whether your website is linked up to your website and vice versa. If you don't fill this field out you will not get the SEO benefits of having a Twitter Account.

Lists

Add people you follow into lists based on subject matter and business type. This means that when you want to carry out research on specific topics or niches you will have some very targeted content to search through. It will allow you to see what's trending within your industry.

Who to Follow?

Be choosy about who you follow. There is a tendency for new Twitter users to use a scatter gun approach to following people, casting the net wide in order to try to get a percentage of those to follow you back. This approach doesn't work because:

A   I can guarantee there will always be less people who follow you back than you have followed

B   Your time-line will be filled with 'noise' – they may be posting rubbish which you are not interested in reading

Be selective about who you want to follow. Choose people within your market sector, peers who are posting about similar topics and where possible follow Twitterers who have a higher reputation than you do. Reputation is gained by the number and reputation of followers and the topics and regularity with which you post. There is a tool called Klout which I will introduce you to later in the book. It is a useful tool, which measures your reputation and suggests users with a higher reputation to follow.

 TOP TIP

Before following a user, look at their bio. This is the biggest marker as to what they are likely to be tweeting about. You will likely be followed by loads of people trying to sell you 5,000 followers, ignore them and certainly don't follow them back. Likewise if someone's profile is incomplete without a banner pic or avatar, don't follow them either. The more engaging the bio the more likely the users' posts will be interesting.

Strategy

You are limited to 140 characters per post on Twitter so you have to be careful and succinct when you post. There are a couple of neat tricks which I would recommend when posting:

1 Post a variety of content consisting of:
   - Tips
   - Company News
   - Industry Related News
   - Try not to ask a question
   - Try to post images, you can also overlay text on images

2   Use URL shorteners such as http://bit.ly. Firstly, you end up with short urls which use up less characters, but also bit.ly provides statistics about links which you shorten using their service so you can see how many clicks each link receives

3   Use #tags within posts; try to use at least one in every post

4   Direct messages to other Twitter users using @tags to start conversations

5   Re-tweet (but don't overdo it)

6   Favourite interesting posts

7   Leave fifteen to twenty characters at the end of your posts. This allows someone to re-tweet your status without it being truncated. This does shorten your character count somewhat but it does mean re-tweets are more punchy

8   Post regularly – if you can at least two or three times per day (during weekdays only if you are a business) at busy times during the day. i.e. 10.30am, 12.30pm and 4.30pm when businesses are likely to be engaging with social media. Posts after midnight will be lost on your audience and become noise

9   Post about content which links back to your website – this is your sales funnel after all so send some traffic back to your own website

Benefits

- Plenty of SEO benefits in linking your Twitter profile up to your website correctly (test for this using Nibbler)
- It's FREE
- Potential for posts to become viral
- Networking opportunities with other businesses
- Twitter shows up in Google Analytics as 'referrals' so you can measure the impact Twitter has on your website traffic

Drawbacks

1 Misuse, there is always going to be misuse and 'trolling' – this won't happen to many organisations but it is useful in larger organisations to have a code of conduct for using social media platforms, to which you ask employees to adhere.

2 Promotion – Twitter, like Facebook, is looking to monetise areas of their service so that it can on the whole remain free to many people. Although Twitter are very transparent about this by showing promoted links with a small orange arrow and precede the post with the words 'promoted by'.

3 Twitter owns your data, so if the service is stopped your posts will disappear with it. My advice is to keep an archive of your posts in a spreadsheet or text file. Firstly this means your content isn't lost if something happens to Twitter but also you can refer back to this archive and recycle it if your inspiration is failing you.

STEP 3

Google+

Google+ is the most recent of the big four platforms to have come to fruition. At the time of writing:

- Google+ had over 300m+ monthly active users
- The average user spends 7 minutes per visit to Google+

How to Register and Set Up and Page

http://www.wikihow.com/Make-a-Google-Plus-Page

Google Product

Google+ is a Google tool therefore, out of the top four social media platforms, it holds the greatest sway when it comes to SEO. Google is the most widely used search engines, which is linked to Google's suite of free products. Not having a Google+ page will be putting your business at a disadvantage over your competitors who do have a Google+ page. Your Google+ page is the official means of getting your business verified by Google, and it links up to other Google tools such as Google Places, Reviews, YouTube and Google Maps (for Directions).

My best piece of advice is to spend time setting your Google+ page up correctly with as much information as possible, and verify your business; whether you choose to actively engage with it or not as a part of your social media marketing campaign.

Branding and Logo

As per Facebook and Twitter you have the option of uploading your company logo and a banner image, so ensure these are consistent.

Website URL

Again, as per Facebook and Twitter, there is a specific field for your website URL. You can use Nibbler to test whether you have linked Google+ up with your website correctly.

Strategy

1   Post a range of media including links, images and videos to make your timeline as interesting as possible
2   Try to create engaging content so that users share and '+1' your posts
3   Google+ also accepts #tags and shortened URLs

Followers

Like Twitter these are people following your page and vice versa. It is also similar to Facebook users liking your page.

Circles

Use circles to organise who you follow and those who follow you. Circles are followers which you can categorise into different groups such as Work, Friends and Acquaintances. Circles are customisable so you can be quite granular. They are similar to Twitter's List feature.

Communities

Communities are groups of Google Users who talk collectively about similar subjects, a bit like a website forum or Groups on Facebook. They are very niche topics and I would recommend joining communities as there are several benefits:

1   Feedback – You can post interesting ideas and blog articles into Communities in order to get feedback from your peer group.
2   Research – Communities discuss topics surrounding your area of expertise, so if you are at a loss about what to blog about or to find some trending topics these are often good places to go to find that information.

Reviews

Invite your customers to leave reviews in the 'About' section of your Google+ Page whenever you sell a product or service. You may have noticed in Google's organic search engine listings that some search results are returned with a star rating underneath the main heading. This is because that company has received a number of positive reviews. There are paid for services which Google references for its reviews however it also uses its own review system. I would imagine that having a number of positive reviews will act as a marker in Google's search engine algorithm as well, so getting positive reviews may help your website's pagerank. You can use these reviews on your own website as testimonials.

Verification Process

This is Google+'s most valuable feature, in my opinion. Google's verification process is actually quite archaic as they send out a unique pin code on a post card to your physical registered address (which can take up to two weeks to arrive). Once verified though a small shield will appear in your Google+ page just above your company name. This is a good indicator that your business is a verified local business and is trustworthy.

⏻ TOP TIP

Ensure your business is verified by Google, however make sure you complete the verification process. A postcard can easily be lost in the post, or if your business has a few employees let your admin team know you are expecting a postcard from Google otherwise it might make it into the recycling pile before it gets to you. Sometimes people don't actually even realise they are going to get a postcard, instead thinking the verification process is completed via email, so make sure you look out for a postcard and follow the instructions on it.

Completing the verification process unlocks additional features on your Google+ page including a map displaying your location with some extra information on it with a verified address for your business. It can only help to serve your website's pagerank.

Downsides

As per Facebook and Twitter, all of the information you are posting onto your Google+ page is owned by Google so should they choose to close the service down then your data will be lost along with the service. Google do deprecate features which they are not monetising so there is always a risk that they might close a service down. Keep an archive of your posts where possible.

The review system can easily be 'trolled' as Google allows unverified users to leave reviews which means one of your competitors can login and leave a negative review if they so wish. However, there is a space for you to respond to a review and normally these kinds of reviews are quite transparent.

It can be a little bit tricky to set up a Google+ page correctly, so take time right from the start to spend sufficient time in understanding the interface and setting your page up. There are plenty of benefits to setting the page up correctly so stick with it. Reference YouTube tutorials when setting up your Google+ page.

 TOP TIP

If you are struggling with setting up and of your social media profiles then engage with an expert to help you set them all up. They will be able to set up your profiles much more efficiently and effectively, and know exactly which bits of information to add and where.

Benefits

- It's free
- Linked to other Google products
- Helps SEO pagerank if linked to your website correctly

STEP 4

LinkedIn

LinkedIn is a great business to business networking tool. It is the more established of the big four social media platforms in terms of how long it has been around for and is perfect for Business to Business networking. At the time of writing:

- LinkedIn had over 275m+ monthly active users
- The average user spends seventeen minutes per month on LinkedIn
- Setting up the personal profile is relatively easy

How to Register and Set Up and Page

http://www.wikihow.com/Use-LinkedIn
http://www.wikihow.com/Create-an-Account-on-LinkedIn
http://www.wikihow.com/Edit-a-Company-Page-on-Linkedin

Your Profile and Business Profile

LinkedIn allows you to set up your own personal profile as well as a separate business profile page. In a way similar to Facebook but your personal profile is much more professional and geared towards other business professionals. The personal profile allows you to add information about your previous employments, education and your skill-set. As per the other platforms you can upload a professional head-shot and a custom background so you can make your LinkedIn profile consistent with your brand image.

Your LinkedIn connections can endorse you for specific skills, and you can invites users to endorse you for skills, which are like personal reviews. But do look at what you've been endorsed for because LinkedIn makes the suggestion and asks your connections to confirm it and LinkedIn isn't always right!

Finally you can link your profile page up to businesses you have worked for via their business page. So, if you work within your own micro-business you can also set up your own business page. This means that if someone searches for you or your brand within LinkedIn they will get one or both in the results. Plus there are the additional SEO benefits from having a business profile page as well. It can be indexed in the various search engines. You can create a link on your business profile back to your website. You can also post updates on your business page as well.

LinkedIn Groups

LinkedIn Groups are discussion forums about specific subject topics. Joining in with conversations on Groups is a great way of raising your profile and visibility. Being a part of a group is also a good means of networking and finding out more about events which are happening in your local area. Groups are a great way of sharing your own expertise by helping others or if you need some advice then this is also a great forum for asking for help.

Getting Sales Leads

The paid for versions of LinkedIn allow for two great features:

1 **See who's viewed your profile** – these may be people who you have already met or people who have looked at your profile with a view to doing business with you therefore they are already pre-

warmed leads and always worthwhile following up. Take a look at their profile and see what area of business they are in, because you never know there may be a great opportunity waiting.

2   **Filter connections** – LinkedIn's search tool allows you to filter profiles by their business demographics which means you can niche down on business with a £1m+ turnover, in London with ten or more employees. This means you can highly target a niche of potential customers and find the right person to speak to within that organisation; doing a small amount of research can go an awfully long way.

Etiquette

 TOP TIP

My biggest tip by far for LinkedIn is for when you are making new connections. The default invite message that LinkedIn creates for you is, 'Hi Rob, James would like to join your LinkedIn network'. Make sure you personalise that message and remind the person where you met them, 'Hi Rob, We met recently at the Gloucestershire Chamber of Commerce breakfast and had an interesting conversation about Social Media in Business. Perhaps we can talk more over coffee as I'd be interested to hear what you might be able to do for my business...Kind regards, James'. It's just a bit more personable and warmer; we are all very busy people so sometimes a gentle jog of the memory helps.

Personally I prefer to connect with people on LinkedIn who I have actually met or with whom I have a strong chance of doing business. Where possible avoid casting the net out on LinkedIn as that is how it will be seen; networking is only the first part of the relationship and setting a good tone from the outset is key.

STEP 5

Content Strategy

The section in this book is not designed to be a 'how to guide' on setting up and using social media platforms. There are plenty of experts out there who can help you to set up your social media platforms if you are struggling. Equally there are thousands of videos on YouTube covering the topic.

If you don't have a social media presence at all you are losing out in 2 ways. Firstly, as we have established in the previous chapters, social media acts as a marker for the search engines. Secondly, a majority of people go straight to Google to search, however there are lots of people who use Twitter, Facebook, LinkedIn and Google+ to search for business(es). By not having a social media presence at all you may be missing out on finding potential partners for your business.

 TOP TIP

At the very least do set up the four social media profiles, even if you don't intend to actively engage with them. You never know, one day you might and your profiles will already be there, ready and waiting.

The really valuable knowledge that I want to share with you is not based around having a social media presence. It is, as you may already have guessed, based around the engagement strategy which you will need to implement once your profiles are set up.

This is broken down into three parts:

1   Content Strategy, which I will demonstrate in this chapter
2   Scheduling Strategy
3   Automation Strategy

I will run through the Scheduling and Automation strategies in the next chapter; I will also introduce some handy tools in the remaining chapters of the book to help with scheduling and automation as well.

What I hope to achieve is to share with you a Social Media Strategy which you can easily implement, and one that will save you valuable time. Time which can be spent working on the areas of your business which are your core competencies.

Essential and Non-Essential Tasks

This is a good time to mention 'essential and non-essential tasks'. Many boot-strapped businesses suffer with a lack of time, but then they also try to save money by doing many non-essential tasks themselves.

An essential task is one in which you, as the business owner, are vital. If you get hit by a bus your business will not be able to function because all of the intellectual property and ability to implement are held within you.

A non-essential task is everything else.

Think about your daily tasks and break them down into a list of essential and non-essential tasks. Now think about this, 'What would it feel like if someone else could do all of your non-essential tasks so you only have to focus on doing the essential tasks?' Could you make more money? Would it be more fun? Would you have more time to focus on your essential tasks?

Many non-essential tasks can be outsourced. You do not have to outsource everything, as this can be quite costly, but over time I would recommend outsourcing as many of your non-essential tasks as possible.

Your website and social media marketing do fit into this criteria because, while it is essential for your business to have them, it is *not* essential for you to be doing the work.

I have digressed.

If you are going to undertake a social media strategy (or someone within your organisation is) the key thing here is that I am going to show you how to do it in an efficient and organised manner which will save you time.

The benefit of implementing your own social media strategy is that it will be you who will be writing your content. You know your target market and your products and services better than anyone after all. What I really want to do is demonstrate that social media doesn't need to take up too much of your time once you have the necessary tools to help you.

One common misunderstanding is thinking that blog posts should be these long, boring white-papers which are thoroughly researched and demonstrate an expert level of skill. Well, that's a load of rubbish. Yes, social media is about content creation and content sharing. However, a blog post need only be a couple of hundred words, including rich content such as a video, podcast, infographic or photo. If it provides valuable tips and insights then that's all it needs to be.

Challenge yourself to spend just fifteen minutes once per week to write a helpful article for your customers. 300 words multiplied by fifty weeks equals 15,000 words. And funnily enough this is the benchmark Google gives for the perfect amount of content on a website to demonstrate authority.

I mention blogging at this stage because your website is going to be your main sales funnel. Therefore when you implement a social media strategy you ultimately want to be driving visitors back to your website.

The Content Strategy

Recently someone showed me a very simple means of creating a content strategy for the coming year. This is specifically for your blog, but you need engaging content on your website to drive traffic from social media.

So, open up Excel, and in the first row at the top of each column add in six to eight topics, in which your business is expert. This could be anything surrounding your products or services, for which you are known by your customers.

Use the fifteen to twenty rows underneath each topic to create titles of blog articles you could write. For example:

Website Design	SEO	Social Media	etc
25 Questions to ask your web developer	What is Google Penguin?	How to develop a social media strategy?	etc
The 7 best tools for testing your website with	What is Meta Data?	etc	etc
What is Wordpress?	etc	etc	etc

Pretty quickly you will have developed 100-150 articles which you can now write throughout the year.

Task Management - ToDoIst

A content strategy is useless without implementation. Use a Task Management tool such as ToDoIst to help you implement your strategy. Put each of your blog article titles in as a separate entry in ToDoIst with a week's gap between each one. You will then receive reminders each week to write an article about a specific topic without having to think about it.

Record Your Article, Pay Someone to transcribe it

If you are worried about how long these might take to write you, or if writing just isn't your forte. Record the article into your smartphone. Most people speak at about 90-100 words per minute, so 300 words is going to be about three minutes of audio. Then use a service such as Fiverr and pay someone a few pounds to transcribe your article for you.

Economies of Scale, Record Articles in Bulk

You could record ten articles in one go, get them transcribed and then post-date the articles when you publish them in your blog. That way, they are drip-fed on a weekly basis and you only have a chunk of work to complete once every ten weeks.

TOP TIP

Try and rotate your subject matter on a regular basis. If your articles are all on the same subject they may become boring.

Social Media

So, you're probably asking, 'Where does social media fit into this?'

I am now going to try and break down what sort of content you should be posting on your social media profiles.

Your Own Website Content

Once you have started to create content you have something tangible, to which site visitors are directed. If you already have lots of products or pages of content on your website then you can also leverage that within your social media posts.

A blog is normally a good way of providing helpful tips back to your customers in a user-friendly format.

Try cutting and pasting your blog article title, and a link to that article into Facebook, Google+, Twitter and LinkedIn and see what happens. You will notice that Facebook and Google+ pull in a preview of your post (title and description) automatically as well as a thumbnail of any images you've posted. In Twitter and Google+ you might want to pop the hashtag symbol in front of a few keywords within your post. And maybe if you've written the article with a specific customer in mind use the @tag in twitter or tag that user in Facebook as well.

Wow, that was easy wasn't it?

Other People's Websites and Industry Related News

You are a fountain of knowledge, but there is also a huge amount of other useful information out there on the web. So, if you find a useful article which you feel might be valuable to your customers or your peers, then share it. Using the same method as highlighted above. Sharing other people's insights is equally as valuable as sharing your own.

I follow several leading industry magazines through my own personal Facebook timeline. Interesting reading for me but also very insightful for my customers. If I see an article which I feel offers value I read it and share it. The beauty of this is that Facebook pushes the articles in front of me; I don't even have to go and find high quality content to share.

Useful Stats, Tips and Quotes

You may not always have the time to write informative articles, or do the research to find other helpful content. Equally your audience may not have the time to read your content.

Sharing Stats, Tips, Quotes and other bits of useful micro-information can demonstrate expertise and grab someone's attention with a very short and succinct post.

Links to Rich Media

Don't forget that Video, Podcasts and Infographics are also very engaging, so posting links to rich media content will engage potential customers. More so if you have created the rich media as this demonstrates your expertise and adds your character and personality to your business.

Retweeting

If you stumble across an interesting tweet then retweet it if you feel it will give your audience value. Again, this is a quick means of generating valuable content for your own social media profile timelines.

Rotate Posts and Post Types

 TOP TIP

Try and use a variety of different post types. If all you do is retweet other people's content pretty soon your audience will get bored. Share a range of different media and post types to create greater engagement.

If you keep an archive of all of your status updates you can recycle older posts which you know had a greater reach or engagement with your audience. In short this means reposting older posts.

If you have an active social media strategy in place, content will disappear from the top of your timeline and any search results quite quickly. Also, new followers may not have seen some of your older posts. So there is nothing wrong with re-using valuable content that you have already posted.

Again, don't overdo this; otherwise your timeline will become repetitive and boring.

To Share Everywhere or not to Share Everywhere?

There are two trains of thought about sharing one post across all four platforms. Some suggest you shouldn't do this in case you have customers who engage with you across multiple platforms; they will see the same posts everywhere. I would argue that there are few people, especially in the SME markets, which will be looking at more than one of your social media platforms.

There is an argument that a variety of different content on the different platforms may have a positive impact on SEO, but it will be marginal. I would only recommend applying a different strategy to each platform if you have the resources.

One shortcut might be to stagger posts on different platforms, even if it's by a day per platform.

Don't Hide Your Message

Another common mistake which people make when developing their website or when creating social media content is to 'hide their message' behind comedy, metaphors, anecdotes and entertainment.

Remain professional at all times especially when using social media. You have to be so succinct when posting updates that your message could easily be misconstrued and be seen as offensive to potential customers. More simply the comedy, metaphor or anecdote will be lost and overlooked.

Scheduling and Automation

The next chapter is on Social Scheduling and Automation. This allows you to create content in bulk once a week or once a month and have a piece of software drip feed your social media content over a period of time.

STEP 6

Scheduling and Automation Strategy

Bigger businesses can afford the expense of bringing in members of a staff to manage their social media strategy. Some organisations even have a member of staff for each social media channel, and even different departments working within the same platform.

Micro businesses and SMEs may not be able to afford this luxury, and so when working within a Bootstrapped business the two key areas of savings are made in terms of money and time. What is the most economical and efficient means of delivering a big business social media strategy on the resources of a micro-business?

For a social media strategy being delivered within a micro-business this is achieved through automation and scheduling.

The Pain of Updating

The biggest pain point for many small businesses is the grunt work required to log in to several social media platforms on an almost daily basis just in order to keep up. It can easily become a full-time job just to carry out the research, format the posts, login to each platform and post an update. And that happens several times a day as well.

We are not looking for a shortcut, because the quality of the content has to remain consistent. What you are aiming to achieve is to create an economy of scale by creating a bulk load of content and updates in one go and then delivering it at the appropriate time on a regular basis.

Your Toolkit

There are software as a service (subscription based) tools available which can help you to do exactly that. In the last four chapters of this book I will introduce the four most commonly used tools individually. These tools are:

1 Sprout Social
2 Hootsuite
3 Buffer
4 Klout

Each of these tools offers capabilities of helping you:

- research suitable topics to post about
- people of influence who you should be connecting with
- analytics tools so you can see how your profiles are performing
- schedule posts and distribute your content at the appropriate time automatically
- shorten long urls automatically

Discipline

One of the more important factors for implementing a successful social media strategy revolves around discipline and planning. Luckily it involves less discipline than logging in daily. Instead I would encourage you to block out a morning or afternoon once a month, that's only four hours, to create your social media content for the month ahead.

Let's say you are aiming to post something 3 times a day during weekdays only. Then that equates to sixty posts per month. That allows for four minutes to research, write and schedule each post. This doesn't include writing the blog articles, however, but if you can then aim to write one blog article per week.

Here is my recommended content mix (per month):

1. Blog Posts – 4
2. Stats, Tips and Quotes – 8
3. Existing Website Product or Service Pages – 8
4. Image Posts – 4
5. Links to YouTube videos (yours or others) – 6

Halfway there already, here are some more suggestions:

1. Industry related news – 8
2. Peer group websites – 6
3. Company announcements – 4
4. Customer Testimonials/Reviews – 6
5. Any other business – 6

Well, very easily that's sixty posts per month. This is just an example so perhaps you can change the regularity of posts and number of posts against each post type to suit your organisation.

Posting Three Times a Day

Three is a nice number but you can post as many or as few times per day as you choose. It is a balancing act. Post too much and you will bore people, and you will likely lose followers. Don't post enough and you won't have an engaging timeline for your followers to read.

That's the reason I choose to post three times a day. By the way, this isn't always possible because sometimes life gets in the way and you can give your social media strategy a day off. This is absolutely 100% OK! Come back to it when you are ready with a fresh perspective and renewed enthusiasm.

Posting three times a day is important because people engage with social media at different times of the day. So my key times are 9.30am, 12.30pm and 4.30pm. These correlate to the morning coffee time, lunch time and just before going home time which are the three most common times when people are procrastinating.

You can use tools like Klout and the premium versions of Sprout Social and Hootsuite to recommend to you the best times to post your status updates if you are unsure about when to post. Consider your target audience.

Remember Your Audience

If your business is all about B2B then you will likely be posting at the same time as me. If most of your customers are in the US, but you are based in the UK, then you will need to adjust your post times to match up with your widest target audience. If you are retail B2C then the best time to announce special offers might be 5pm-9pm in the evening. Or if your audience are hard core gamers, 4am.

IN SUMMARY

1   Set aside fifteen minutes per week to write a blog post
2   Block out a morning or afternoon once per month from your calendar to research and produce sixty posts for the coming month
3   Add these posts into one of the scheduling tools recommended earlier in this chapter

And throughout the rest of the month don't forget to:

1   Engage with your followers
2   Reply to direct messages
3   Provide insights, tips and advice

You will find those last three points much easier to undertake and much more enjoyable because the bulk of your social media strategy has already been automated and scheduled. It's the last three points, which create real engagement with your followers. This will create real leverage from your social media profiles and hopefully you will start to see steady organic growth in terms of the number of followers you are engaging and the amount of traffic being driven to your own website.

As a bonus this strategy will help to free up some time for you to focus on your core competencies and to drive your business forward.

STEP 7

Sprout Social

All of the four tools which I am going to demonstrate have either a free version, whether that's on a perpetual use basis or on a short term-trial (fourteen days) or they have a premium version. My recommendation would be to try the free trial for all four tools and then choose the one which you feel will benefit your organisation the most. Each tool has its own merits, so it is down to personal choice really as to which one you prefer to use.

My scheduling and automation weapon of choice is Sprout Social. There are a couple of neat add-ons which Sprout Social has got which make the whole process of scheduling and automating your social media content very straightforward. My intention is to be able to provide a brief introduction into the tool and the features of Sprout Social which I find the most useful.

Sprout Social has a thirty-day free trial and I would thoroughly recommend the paid-for version of their application. With the cheapest package of their paid for service you are able to add up to ten social media platforms (Google, Facebook, Twitter and LinkedIn) which is ample for most micro and small business. You can add multiple profiles on each platform if you have several different accounts for your organisation, or a personal and business twitter account for example.

Within Sprout Social you can set up teams so that multiple people can manage your social media profiles. You can assign tasks to specific users to spread the load somewhat.

Sprout Social's control panel is divided into six sections:

Messages

This is a feed of your messages for ALL profiles you have added in one single timeline. This allows you to reply to direct messages and see who is now following you all from one interface. Sprout Social recently added a Smart Inbox, which shows you how many interactions you have received over the previous eight weeks and prompts you to check them off like a task list.

I find this incredibly useful because it displays new followers biography so you can very quickly gage whether your new follower is likely to be publishing high quality content versus those who are just spamming and selling followers for example (tip: don't follow spammers!). Also, you can see their location, so if they are a local business, with whom you might want to engage.

⏻ TOP TIP

Follow people within a similar peer group and similar interests or businesses who you may want to do business with in the future. Social Media is about engagement so do utilise these feature to keep on top of your new followers and to answer any questions which are raised.

Tasks

If you have multiple people within your organisation linked to Sprout Social then you can use the tasks panel to view any tasks assigned to you.

Feed

This is a timeline summary of all of the people who you are following. This is very useful if you want to retweet other experts' posts and saves time logging into each account individually and manually searching through reams of content to find high-quality content.

 TOP TIP

Social media guru, Minter Dial, provided me with this invaluable tip. Minter introduced me to a great social media research tool called Feedly – https://feedly.com – which is a news feed aggregation service. You can arrange feeds by categories based around your favourite industry-related magazines. The best part is you can import your Feedly into Sprout Social which means you can have all of your social media research fed directly into Sprout Social. You can then share, publish and comment on this content directly from Sprout Social without having to use any other third party tools; a huge time saving.

Publishing

Once you have set up your Sprout Queue (see later in the chapter) you can start to add posts to your queue. The publishing section allows you to view the posts you have lined up in your Sprout Queue and edit, delete or move them. This is useful if you have created a month of content and then need to remove something because it is now irrelevant or move it to the start of the queue if it becomes important.

Discovery

The discovery section on Sprout Social is made up of three sections, Suggestions, Cleanup and Smart Search. The suggestions feature give you a list of potential accounts to follow. This includes those who are following you and you are not following back, and a second list of those who you've had conversations with.

The cleanup tool allows you to cleanse your followers of those who are not active on twitter and who do not follow you back. This allows you to engage with those users who are more active on Twitter.

The smart search allows you to enter keywords based around your industry and pick out new users to follow. You can then save these searches and come back to it later via a quick link.

Reports

As with any strategy you need to analyse how well your social media strategy is working for you. The reports section provides some graphical reporting about your user demographics and their engagement over the previous seven, fourteen, thirty, sixty and ninety days which is great for giving detailed reports or identifying which campaigns have been the most successful.

The Compose Feature

The Compose feature within Sprout Social is one of its more powerful tools. You can cut and paste website URLs directly into the compose tool; it is at this point where the magic happens. It automatically downloads the Page Title, Page Description and a preview of the images on that page of content. Basically it writes your status updates for you. You can then customise it with your own @tags and #tags.

TOP TIP

Website URLs tend to be quite long. Sprout Social allows you to link up your Bit.ly account with Sprout Social. Bit.ly is a URL Shortening tool which takes long URLs (e.g. http://coconutstrategy.com/blog/2014/12/7-best-tools-for-testing-your-website) and shortens them (e.g. https://bit.ly/g65Hyk8l). Saving valuable characters in Twitter.

You can choose an image to go with your post which Sprout Social automatically pulls in from the web page you are previewing. Which is great if you've added images to your blog posts. Alternatively you can upload a custom photo of your choice. The compose tool allows you to choose which of your social media platforms you would like to send your post to.

Sprout Queue

At the bottom of the compose tool you will see the Scheduling tools built into Sprout Social. You have the option to post straight away, or you can add the post to the beginning or end of your Sprout Queue. Alternatively you can pre-schedule posts to land on a specific date and time, for example if you've got an event coming up and want to automate posts a month, week or day before your event and even during the event as well.

Your queue is governed by your Sprout Queue settings (click on the small cog wheel in the top right hand corner of your browser window and click on Sprout Queue). You will see a weekly timeline against each of the profiles you have added. So you can start to customise how many times a day you want to post and at what times during the day. As we saw earlier, I like to post three times a day during weekdays at 9.30, 12.30pm and 4.30pm, when people are likely to be procrastinating.

The more expensive Sprout Social packages actually choose the best times to post your content for you. This is very useful if you have a more international audience and content is time zone specific.

Browser Plugin

The Chrome Browser Plugin for Sprout Social is quite simply brilliant. I like to share industry related news which I find either through my own Facebook timeline or industry related magazines online. You can find the plugin downloads either within the Sprout Social settings or on their website. Google 'Sprout Social Browser Plugin'. When the plugin is installed, browse to an article you want to share and click on the Sprout Social icon in the top-right corner of your browser. It does all of the URL importing and URL shortening automatically for you. Once you have done this a few times, it can take the process of logging into each social media platform and sharing content from several minutes down to about ten to twenty seconds. A huge time saving especially, like me, when you have to produce eighty or more social posts per month.

STEP 8

Hootsuite

https://hootsuite.com/

Hootsuite sports a thirty day free trial as well as many similar features to Sprout Social. I will try to break down the main differences between the two platforms so that you have a fair comparison. However, I would thoroughly recommend making use of the free trials on offer and testing out several different tools for yourself in order to gauge which one suits you best.

Number of Profiles

Hootsuite's basic package allows you to manage up to 100 social media profiles, ten times the number of Sprout Social. This might be good for agencies with a number of client profiles to manage or for larger businesses with multiple departmental profiles, or a business with a number of diverse products or brands within their organisation.

Content Scheduling

Sprout Social allows you to schedule as much content as you would like so technically you could front load a year's content. Hootsuite only allows you to schedule up to 350 messages in your campaign plan. 350 messages is plenty by the way for most organisations and represents several months' content for the average business.

In the basic version of Hootsuite, it will choose the best time to post your messages. With Sprout Social you have to upgrade to the more expensive package(s) in order to get this facility; Hootsuite does this automatically.

User Management

Hootsuite's collaboration and user management is more diverse in functionality than Sprout Social. You can manage each of your social media profiles by department, brand and region. This allows for your social media strategy to be more granular. If you have a larger organisation Hootsuite is better equipped to deal with that and team working. You can assign tasks to others within Sprout Social but it is geared more towards smaller organisations. Hootsuite is an Enterprise level solution in that respect.

Browser Plugins

Hootsuite has browser plugins available for Chrome and Firefox so you can achieve some of the same time-saving benefits experienced with Sprout Social.

Archiving

 TOP TIP

Twitter now provides a facility to download an archive of your feed. From an IP ownership perspective this is great but you need to be disciplined in downloading that archive on a regular basis, especially if you are posting messages regularly. Hootsuite has an inbuilt feature for archiving messages which Sprout Social currently doesn't. This is very powerful from a disaster recovery process but it also means that if you haven't saved your posts as a part of your social media strategy...well, now you can.

Advanced Features

There are some advanced features which are available within the enterprise level plans on Hootsuite. These are targeted at businesses with 500+ employees and so are not aimed at SMEs.

If your business is global, you can geo-target messages and schedule posts to be delivered at different times depending on times zone. This is important if you have any subscription based products and want to ensure your content is delivered and shared at the same time (e.g. 9am) throughout the world. If you are a startup, this probably isn't important to start out with. It's useful to be aware of advanced features so you don't have to migrate from one application to another later on.

The more expensive options come with a dedicated account manager with enhanced technical support. Hootsuite can also filter your messages and check them for compliance.

Platform Compatibility

Sprout Social focuses on Facebook, Twitter, LinkedIn and Google+. Hootsuite is hooked up to a wider variety of social media platforms; some of the more widely known platforms includes:

- Instagram
- Flipboard
- Reddit
- Tumblr
- Vimeo
- Mailchimp
- SugarCRM
- Marketo

- SalesForce
- Zendesk

If you take a look at the App Directory on Hootsuite you will see all of the different third party applications (currently numbering 115) that work with Hootsuite. Having a multitude of different social media profiles spread across a variety of platforms would be one way of leveraging the 100 profiles which you can link to your Hootsuite account. Some of the third party apps are paid for services and some are free.

For me this presents a much greater opportunity to raise your profile than Sprout Social. This would allow you to create a profile across multiple platforms and be able to distribute content to those platforms in a more automated fashion which can only help to raise your profile.

Engagement

 TOP TIP

The biggest benefit both Hootsuite and Sprout Social appear to have over Buffer lies within the engagement features and the ability to engage with your audience. Social media strategy isn't just about content distribution it is actually about engagement with potential customers and people in general. Many people get caught up in the humdrum of research and content creation and often forget about engagement.

The whole purpose of scheduling and automating the research and creation process is to free up more time for you to engage with people and nurture relationships with customers which will be invaluable to you in the future. Social media is all about conversations, partnerships and engagement.

STEP 9

Buffer

https://bufferapp.com

Buffer is capable of a great deal of what Sprout Social and Hootsuite are capable of. There is a free trial available so that you can try before you buy and I would recommend you do this. With Buffer's small business package you can connect up to twenty-five profiles and up to five team members which is plenty for most small businesses.

One of the features which I like the most about Buffer is the approval processes. It has very powerful team collaboration built inherently within the app; with specific administration rights at a very granular level.

RSS Feed Import

You can import up to fifteen RSS feeds directly into Buffer per profile. This allows for you to shortcut your research processes by bringing industry related news directly into the app which presents a significant benefit over Sprout Social and Hootsuite where the research process is manual.

Security

Buffer have implemented two factor authentication which enhances security; two factor authentication is implied which means that Buffer is inherently more secure than the other two platforms. Depending on the nature of your business, security might be an important element of your business and protecting yours or your customer's privacy.

Scheduling and Buffering

These are standard features within Buffer. The features listed above are all in the Buffer for Business Plan. They have an Awesome Plan. The Awesome Plan is actually the cheaper plan and is geared towards freelancers and solopreneuers. The fact that it is called the awesome plan is pretty awesome though!

Browser Extensions

Buffer has extensions for Chrome, Safari and Firefox.

Native Mobile Apps

There are iOS and Android apps available for Buffer, as per Hootsuite and Sprout Social.

Third Party Integrations

Buffer has one major benefit over Sprout Social in that is it integrated with over fifty social media platforms at present. Slightly less than Hootsuite. Buffer is linked to apps such as:

- Feedly
- Tweetcaster
- Zapier
- InstaPaper
- Digg
- Twitter (obviously)
- WordPress
- Paper.ly
- SideBar

⏻ TOP TIP

Zapier is a great SaaS product which I mentioned earlier on in the book. Zapier is a business automation tool which handles micro-tasks. i.e. when someone tweets @RobinMWaite with the hashtag support then add a support ticket in Zendesk. If you don't understand it then ask your web developer or similar techie wizard to look into how Zapier might be able to help your business. Embrace cloud based solutions as they will definitely save you time and money.

IN SUMMARY (BENEFITS)

- Sprout Social – Focus on main four platforms, ease of use, it works really well
- Hootsuite – Enterprise level, most app integrations of the three tools, archiving feature
- Buffer – Security, variety of app integrations, import RSS feeds

STEP 10

Klout

https://klout.com/home

I'll kick off with the negative; Klout is limiting in the fact that it is not connected to as many social media platforms as Sprout Social, Buffer and Hootsuite. However, what it does, it does incredibly well. It is also a free tool, which makes it invaluable based on some of the features it has.

Klout Score

Klout's most prominent feature is the Klout Score. Your Klout score demonstrates how influential you are (on Twitter mostly) in terms of the connections you are making, relevance of content and regularity that you publish content. Following people with a greater reputation score than you will only help to raise your reputation on Twitter and your Klout score; but only if you then engage with those people on relevant topics of conversation.

Research Tool

When you first setup Klout it invites you to add in a set of specific keywords which are relevant to your organisation's core products and services. Once set up and logged into your control panel you can then select one of your keywords and Klout automatically displays your personalised daily suggestion, including; three people with a higher Klout score than you who you might choose to follow.

TOP TIP

Remember that social media is about Relevancy, Automation, Reputation and Engagement.

Klout then recommends three topics or pages of content, about which you might want to post a message, making the research process very simple indeed. Don't share everything that Klout suggests though, as it can sometimes recommend content which isn't relevant to your business. Do get into the habit of reading any content which you are about to share to make sure it is in congruency with your overall content strategy.

You can then move onto the next keyword and do the same. So if you have a dozen keywords setup within Klout you can very quickly and easily produce several days of scheduled messages and engage with other Twitter users.

 TOP TIP

Do some keyword research first and see what keywords others are using so that your subject matter is relevant and on point. Otherwise you may lose credibility if your posts do not get any traction once published.

Scheduling

Klout does scheduling very well, it automatically suggests the best time(s) to schedule your posts. The scheduling tool is very easy to understand and use, enabling you to research and create scheduled content within a matter of two or three clicks. I find this most useful if I am working remotely or while travelling and don't have access to my full suite of resources in the office.

Measure

The analytics on Klout is wonderfully simple. The report provides a timeline of your Klout score over the previous three months.

I've found this to be a good overview of how productive you have been throughout your social media campaign. For example, I went on holiday recently and forgot to schedule my social media content while I was away. This meant that I came back to work to find my Klout score has fallen off a cliff from sixty-eight back down to forty-four in the space of two weeks. It takes a lot of time, patience and discipline to achieve a score of sixty-plus on Klout so it was quite disappointing.

It acts as a reminder though as to why scheduling and automation are so important when it comes to social media, or at least a collective mind-set between your team members, to update social media if one of you is away on holiday or off sick.

Use in Conjunction with Other Tools

I wouldn't recommend using Klout on its own unless you are solely going to be using Twitter to drive your social media campaign. On its own it has some merits but I have found it gives the best advantage when being used in conjunction with one of the other three tools; Sprout Social, Buffer or Hootsuite. It will add to the variety of content you are posting on Twitter and helps to engage with users with a higher reputation than your own, in order to improve your Klout Score.

CLOSING THOUGHTS

I hope that you have enjoyed reading *Online Business Startup* as much as I have enjoyed writing it. Starting out on any business journey is an exciting prospect. However, taking the leap of faith can be extremely daunting for the uninitiated. Someone once told me, 'The net doesn't appear until you've jumped!' And this is one of the truest things I've ever heard. I have helped numerous business owners face challenges during their careers, and I include my own business within that list, but deciding to startup or even change direction requires strength, courage and most importantly stamina.

Online Business Startup is designed to be a guide and not a bible as there is only so much that can be compiled into one book. I have years of experience in business and still draw on other people's expertise in the form of reading books, business coaches and mentors which build my skillset further. Never be afraid to ask for help in business if you are struggling to make a decision or are unsure of where to turn next as there is always someone out there who has done what you've done, been through what you've been through and has strived to achieve similar objectives.

Online Business Startup will hopefully have set you on the right path to starting up a successful online venture. You will now face challenges, worry and stress. Perhaps you will be tired, feel like you are on a rollercoaster and not know what's going to happen next. You may even go through feelings of disillusion.

On the flip-side…

You will also go through the good times, excitement and growth. The feeling of on-boarding your first customer and telling your friends and family about it. Elation when your first payments start coming in and testimonials and reviews from your customers for a job well done. The immense satisfaction knowing that you are helping your customers or your customer's businesses to grow.

You will have a sense of ownership because people want the products or services you are now selling online. Once upon a time these were nothing more than ideas. You will have flexibility to help others and do so creatively.

One of the biggest values I have found from running my own business is the sense of adventure that I experienced as a child and the free-reign to imagine where this adventure will take me. And I can see in my clients what it is like to start to imagine what they can do with their own businesses.

And hopefully you will experience the freedom of working for yourself, spending more time with your family and enjoy watching your children grow up.

THE NEXT STEPS...

If you are a business professional, the owner of an established business or a funded startup and in need of advice about your branding, business, web or content marketing strategy I offer a free 60 minute coaching session.

You can email me personally at robin@coconut-group.com. I run regular 1-to-1 workshops with business owners covering branding, content strategy, business strategy, video marketing and social media.

If you particularly enjoyed the book and found it helpful then please leave a review on Amazon. This will help others in your field or in similar circumstances to make an informed decision about buying Online Business Startup.

For more details on my coaching programs, to receive regular coaching updates or to join the Online Business Startup accountability group on Facebook please visit: http://robinwaite.com/OBS

Here you can share your tips and experiences with other Business Startups and I will be happy to answer any questions you might have in regards to the book and business strategy generally.

RESOURCES

Websites:

- http://www.thesellabilityscore.com/learning-center
- http://www.forbes.com/sites/martinzwilling/2013/09/06/10-tips-for-building-the-most-scalable-startup/
- http://www.inc.com/articles/2010/05/building-a-sellable-business.html
- http://10steps2.com/scalable-business/
- http://www.entrepreneurhandbook.co.uk/how-to-make-your-business-scalable/
- http://www.statisticbrain.com/startup-failure-by-industry/
- http://www.onlinedesignuk.co.uk/odblog/index.php/web-design/the-105m-website-the-most-expensive-website-ever
- http://www.ebizmba.com/articles/search-engines
- http://read-able.com/
- http://articles.bplans.com/5-critical-mistakes-to-avoid-when-creating-your-logo/
- http://www.smashingmagazine.com/2009/06/25/10-common-mistakes-in-logo-design/
- Wrap Bootstrap – http://www.wrapbootstrap.com
- Theme Forest – http://themeforest.net/
- W3 Layouts – http://w3layouts.com/
- Nibbler – http://nibbler.silktide.com
- PageScoring – http://www.pagescoring.com/website-speed-test/]
- GTMetrix – http://gtmetrix.com
- Pingdom – http://tools.pingdom.com/fpt/
- SortSite – http://try.powermapper.com/

- W3C Validation Tool – http://validator.w3.org/
- Wave Accessibility Tool – http://wave.webaim.org/
- https://support.twitter.com/articles/49309-using-hashtags-on-twitter

READING LIST

Title	What's it About	Read?
.Net Magazine	The voice of website design providing tips and tricks, design ideas and showcasing the latest in emerging web technologies.	
The Chimp Paradox Dr. Steve Peters	The Acclaimed Mind Management Programme to Help You Achieve Success, Confidence and Happiness.	
The Lean Entrepreneur Brant Cooper, Patrick Vlaskovits	How Visionaries Create Products, Innovate with New Ventures, and Disrupt Markets.	
Contagious Jonah Berger	Why Things Catch On.	
Zappos – Delivering Happiness Tony Hsieh	A Path to Profits, Passion, and Purpose.	
The Art of Being Brilliant Andy Copy, Andy Whittaker	Being brilliant, successful, and happy isn't about dramatic change, it's about finding out what really works for you and doing more of it.	
Built to Sell John Warrilow	Creating a Business That Can Thrive Without You	
Rework Jason Fried, David Heinemeier Hansson	a different kind of business book one that explores a new reality	

Title	What's it About	Read?
Entrepreneur Revolution Daniel Priestley	How to Develop Your Entrepreneurial Mindset and Start a Business That Works	
Made to Stick Chip Heath, Dan Heath	Why do some ideas thrive while others die?	
The Lean Startup Eric Reis	How Today's Entrepreneurs Use Continuous Innovation to Create Radically Successful Businesses	
Pitch Anything Oren Klaff	An Innovative Method for Presenting, Persuading, and Winning the Deal	

ABOUT THE AUTHOR

Robin Waite is Business Strategy Expert and co-founder of a successful Online Strategy Agency in the UK. He has helped over 200 businesses create change and growth within their organisation since 2004.

Robin has personally delivered discovery sessions in Business, Online and Social Media Strategy to over 1,000 business owners during that time.

Robin gained a degree in Business Management whilst working as a Systems Analyst; this has provided him with a unique way of seeing businesses from *outside-of-the-box*. More recently Robin won a CPD Award from the Institute of Direct and Digital Marketing.

Robin now specialises in creating growth and scalability within established SMEs turning over £500k+ through a tailored programme of coaching, workshops and practical implementation.

For more information please see: http://about.me/robin.waite or follow me on Twitter: @RobinMWaite

30029839R00149

Printed in Great
Britain
by Amazon